WILL YOUNG

WILL YOUNG
THE BIOGRAPHY

ERICA McPHEE

Michael O'Mara Books Ltd

First published in 2005 by
Michael O'Mara Books Limited
9 Lion Yard
Tremadoc Road
London SW4 7NQ

A CIP catalogue record for this book is available from
the British Library.

This book has not been approved, licensed or endorsed by
Will Young or his management company.

ISBN 1-84317-175-9

1 3 5 7 9 10 8 6 4 2

Designed and typeset by E-Type

Printed and bound in Great Britain by Clays Ltd, St Ives plc

www.mombooks.com

Contents

Author's Acknowledgements

A huge thank you to Will fan Jo Hoare, who pointed me in the direction of some great sources, and was every bit as excited as me about all things Will.

Thank you to Ray Kibeiro and Clare Robinson simply for making me laugh a lot!

A massive thank you to Kate Gribble at Michael O'Mara Books for being so calm, understanding and helpful throughout the writing of the book. It was, and is, hugely appreciated. Thanks also to the rest of the team at Michael O'Mara Books.

Thank you to Gill Smith for all the tea and encouragement, and to Alex Smith for being so lovely. Also, Annie – welcome to the world!

Thanks to all Will Young fans for their inspiration. Although he fully deserves such fans, he is lucky to have such incredible supporters.

And finally, a big thanks to the man himself: I wish him all the luck in the world for the future.

Erica McPhee, September 2005

Picture Acknowledgements

Introduction

In February 2002, a true star was born when William Robert Young was crowned the winner of the first ever *Pop Idol*.

The well-spoken Berkshire native wasn't the obvious winner, and in fact only just managed to scrape through his first audition, after initially failing to impress the judges with his scruffy outfit and quirky rendition of the disco classic 'Blame It On The Boogie'.

It was only further down the line, following his well-executed argument with Simon Cowell and some amazing vocal performances, that he finally started to get noticed. But with fierce competition from the likes of baby-faced Gareth Gates and sexy Sarah Whatmore, few would have predicted in those early days that the good-natured politics graduate would walk away with the *Pop Idol* prize.

However, as the weeks went by in the competition, Will went from strength to strength, consistently proving himself to be a serious contender for the much-desired record contract and management deal. For despite his recently acquired degree, singing was what Will had dreamed of doing his entire life – and his passion shone through in each and every show.

When it came to the crunch, on 9 February 2002, 4.6 million people voted for the posh lad with the incredible voice to win the singing contest that had gripped the nation. Sceptics were quick to dismiss reality-TV-show stars as a flash in the pan in the music industry, but since that day Will has gone on to prove them wrong time and time again.

From his debut single 'Evergreen'/'Anything Is Possible' smashing sales records – it sold an incredible 1.1 million copies in its first week alone – to his debut album *From Now On* shifting over three-quarters of a million copies to date, Will has defied everyone who said he was simply the product of a television phenomenon, who wouldn't survive without the show that made him.

Will's second album, the critically acclaimed *Friday's Child*, sold over 200,000 copies in its first week of release. With this outstanding achievement, Will proved to everyone that he was here to stay. Even the super-critical Simon Cowell couldn't hold back from praising the impressive collection, saying: 'I have to say, Mr Young, this is a *great* record. You sound great on it. Good production. Could be a number one record. I like it a lot.' Hard-won commendation indeed. And Cowell went on to add: 'I'd have given the first album seven out of ten. I would give this album nine out of ten.' It was a view mirrored by dozens more critics and endorsed by the hundreds of thousands of fans who rushed out to buy Will's latest musical offering.

Will has also enjoyed massive success across Europe, where he has scooped numerous Top Five hits. In Italy, he is a style icon, and time and again he has graced the pages of that country's leading fashion magazines. But he's not just a pretty face. Will has also scooped several awards, including two coveted BRITs and an Ivor Novello, which recognizes outstanding songwriting talent. Yet somehow, in the midst of all this craziness, Will has managed to remain startlingly down to earth.

It is in part this refreshing, straightforward approach to

life that has endeared him to his millions of fans. Will has embarked on several sell-out tours during his career, all of which have garnered incredible reviews, with Victoria Newton in the *Sun* enthusing: 'Will Young proved he's our biggest male star next to Robbie Williams as he kicked off his British tour. In trademark ripped jeans and cap, Will captivated the sell-out crowd at St David's Hall, Cardiff, with his mix of charisma and shyness.' The *South Wales Echo* commented: 'There's a reason critics are calling him the next George Michael. Not only can the boy sing, but when it comes to stage presence and charisma, he'd put the majority of so-called "authentic" musicians to shame. He performed all his hits as well as songs from the acclaimed [second] album, including "Your Game" – and the audience loved it.' Who can argue with that?

But Will's talents aren't just confined to music. He achieved one of his lifetime ambitions when he appeared on the West End stage in 2002, following in the footsteps of Roger Moore and Kylie Minogue by guest-starring in *The Play What I Wrote*. And in November 2005 he makes his big-screen acting debut in the film *Mrs Henderson Presents*, playing Bertie, the star performer of a London theatre. Will received much praise from his fellow cast mate, acting legend Dame Judi Dench, for his role in the £10 million movie, and he plans to do plenty more acting in the future.

In a showbiz world where you are defined by how many magazines you appear in, or how many people sell kiss-and-tell stories about you, Will has managed to remain best known for his talent, rather than the gossip he generates – something which he has consciously set out to do, and which is a considerable achievement in today's celebrity-obsessed culture. You won't find Will rolling around the pavement outside a celeb-packed party, or getting into fist-fights with photographers – because despite his celebrity status, he would still rather go down the pub with his mates than hang out at a pretentious party. 'Even when I went into the [*Pop Idol*] competition, I never thought, "I want to be famous to go to premieres and ride in a limousine." I just wanted to sing,' he admits.

When it comes to his professional life, too, Will is a man who won't be swayed by others, but instead holds true to his own ideals and personal aims. As a musical artist, it is all too easy to be pushed around and told what to do by your advisors, but Will is far from simply being a reality-TV pop puppet. He has managed to retain a large amount of control over his career and has refused to compromise in any way. He reveals: 'I'm stubborn. I'm quite prepared to have a big row.'

It is this determination to stick to his guns and not transform into another identikit pop star that has made him popular with people of all ages, and from all walks of life – including the British royal family, who have personally requested that he perform for them on several occasions.

It's certainly been a roller-coaster three years for Will, since *Pop Idol* turned him into an overnight success. This book charts his rise to fame, from shy student to one of the biggest stars in the UK today, and describes the hopes, fears, perils and passions that Will has experienced at every turn. Be it winning the award for Rear of the Year, working hard for charity (he is the patron of a number of organizations, from Mencap to Women's Aid), coming out to a national newspaper, or writing hit songs which seem destined to endure for many decades to come, Will's life is full of unique experiences which have made him the man he is today. It's undoubtedly been an unforgettable journey.

So hold on to your hats, ladies and gentlemen, as we take a ride through the life and times of Mr William Young. It's quite a trip, but as you'll no doubt agree, it's safe to say that this is just the beginning for one of Britain's brightest rising stars.

CHAPTER ONE

The Young Will Young

Will Young was born on 20 January 1979, ten minutes before his twin brother Rupert, making him the middle Young child. The twins' early days were a nerve-racking time for their parents – dad Robin, the company director of an engineering firm, and their nursery gardener mum, Annabel – as the babies were born six weeks prematurely.

However, thankfully the twins made it through those difficult first few weeks, and thereafter began to thrive. They grew up to be healthy, strong boys who, according to Robin, spent much of their time fighting each other. 'The boys like to say that one of them was born with a black eye. They are very close now, but my memory is of them constantly scrapping. They certainly carried on fighting through their younger years. They were always at it.

'The last fight I remember was 30 feet under the sea off the Great Barrier Reef in Australia, a few years ago when they were scuba-diving. They started having a fight on the seabed when one of them wanted to go up to the surface and the other one objected.'

Will himself recalls another huge ruck with Rupert. 'We used to have huge bust-ups. The worst was when he shot me with an air rifle. I was about sixteen, it was the summer holiday and I would practise basketball on the tennis court. I heard a window open. I looked around and saw the nozzle of the air rifle peek out of the window. And he shot me in the leg and shouted, "Don't wake me up again!" and slammed the window. After that it kicked off big time …'

Annabel liked to dress the boys in identical clothes – much to their dismay – but as they were non-identical they could never get away with duping people into thinking they were each other. 'It's really good having a twin, but we have never been so alike that we could pretend to be each other,' says Will, somewhat sadly. 'A lot of twins have that extrasensory perception thing where they can tell what the other's thinking, even when they are apart. But it's quite boring, because Rupert and I aren't like that.'

Robin says that the boys are also very different when it comes to their personalities. 'William didn't conform but he wasn't an outright rebel either – he left that to his brother,' Will's dad recalls. 'Will was good at not being found out, quietly making a stand. Rupert did William's rebelling for him. They're very different characters but in some ways they're two parts of one whole. They complement each other – if one excels in one area, the other will move up in another. At school, if one did French, the other would do German, and if one favoured long-distance running, the other would do sprinting.'

Despite their bickering, Will says that he and Rupert got on well growing up, and they're still very close today. 'It's brilliant because you have an ally in everything you do,' Will says of being a twin. 'We both had a fierce protectiveness of each other. When we went through boarding school it was great to have someone else there. We were in the same houses and I always had someone to play with. I can't imagine what it must be like to be an only child.'

The pair were brought up, alongside their older sister Emma, in Hungerford, a pretty historical market town in Berkshire, which smacks of old-fashioned values. The children had a privileged upbringing and lived in a beautiful £500,000 house with a huge garden, where they loved nothing better than playing with the family pets. 'I had a fortunate upbringing, and my parents are wonderfully eccentric, which has rubbed off on me,' Will explains happily.

Will and Rupert were feisty boys, and while Will was the better behaved of the two and was generally considered to be a polite young man, he also had a naughty side. As well as recalling Will's bizarre taste for the family dog's food, his dad remembers a particular incident when the boys were four years old. 'We were outside their room listening to them open Christmas presents, and out of the blue came Will's remark: "That bastard Santa didn't bring me any Lego."'

Will knew his own mind from a young age and was strong-willed. Despite being a lot shyer than he is these days, he was still happy to have his say when it came to the crunch. For example, when a surgeon suggested that Will's crooked jaw should be broken and reset, Will angrily rebuffed the offer. 'He refused. There was no arguing with him,' reveals Robin.

Will toyed with the idea of being a vet when he was a boy, before deciding that he 'wasn't clever enough'. He loved to entertain and always suspected that he might end up on the stage, but fame was never something he craved. His first taste of performing for an audience came when he was four years old and attending Kingsbury Hill School, when he got the chance to play … a fir tree. He was trussed up in a green velvet outfit and he had just one line to say, which he can still remember today: 'As time went by the beautiful princess grew into a lovely girl.' Learning lyrics later in life was never going to be a problem.

Despite being a little reserved, Will later sang in the choir when he and Rupert attended the upmarket Horris Hill Prep School, near Newbury, Berkshire, from the ages of eight to thirteen. This privileged education would set you back around £13,000 a year today, and Will and Rupert certainly didn't want for anything.

Will was a good pupil, but there was one thing that he just couldn't get the hang of, no matter how hard he tried – cricket. He claims to have been useless at it … as he was always scared of being hit by the ball. However, that small failing hasn't stopped Horris Hill's headmaster, Nigel Chapman, from singing the young Will's praises. 'Will was a good all-rounder and head chorister while he was here,' he reports.

Will and Rupert's next stop was the prominent Wellington College, widely considered to be one of the best schools in the country. It currently costs around £18,000 per year and boasts 750 boys and fifty girls on the school roll.

Any hopes that Will might have had of cutting his musical teeth at Wellington, in a specifically mainstream capacity, were out the window: the school favoured cello playing and classical music above pop classics. Will himself learnt piano from the age of nine, until he reached thirteen and new hobbies took over. 'He learnt the piano when he was nine,' confirms Robin. 'But after a few years he got a bit bored until he started learning more interesting stuff.'

Will was a keen runner, and dreamed of making it to the Olympics and running the 400 metres one day. He could complete the distance in around fifty seconds: in the Olympics they average forty-three seconds, so it was an achievable goal for the ambitious young man. He was keen to train himself to Olympic standard – but soon got sidetracked. Nevertheless, he is still an enthusiastic runner today, and regularly jogs to keep fit.

Having been a quiet child (he says that shyness runs in his family), it was in Will's teen years that he really began to come out of his shell, and he became increasingly outgoing as he grew older. He was soon giving speeches in assemblies and entertaining friends with jokes. The more positive the feedback he received, the more his confidence grew – and the more he realized that his future lay in performing. But his cheeky manner sometimes got him into trouble, and he admits ruefully that the worst thing ever written in his school reports by one of his teachers was, 'My heart sank when I learnt William was in my class.'

While at Wellington, Will appeared in several school productions, but reveals that he always felt slightly awkward about his thespian activities, and was never totally comfortable being the centre of attention. Luckily for Will, however, his abilities stretched beyond the stage, for as well as his performing skills, Will was also a keen and talented sportsman. He became captain of Wellington's basketball and athletics teams, and represented his school in football, rugby, triple jump and long jump too. Yet his love of the arts and sport didn't stop him working hard, and he eventually left school with an impressive ten GCSEs.

Nevertheless, despite his good grades, Will then spent much of his time as a sixth-form student having fun with his mates. He walked away with disappointing A Level results. 'He wasn't interested in passing exams – he was more interested in experimentation,' explains Will's dad Robin. 'He was very disappointed with his A Level grades, and he enrolled to retake them at Oxford sixth-form college.'

Will took a part-time job as a waiter, at the Grand Café in Oxford, to pay his way through doing his retakes. 'He set himself a target and that's what he wanted to achieve. He's a man who sets his own objectives and he went for it,' says Robin.

While completing his A Level retakes, Will became interested in environmental issues and got caught up in some local campaigning in Oxford ... but he hadn't actually let his college tutors know about it. 'I was eighteen and a member of the Eco Society, and I was making this documentary about the demonstrations to try and stop the Newbury bypass,' Will explains. 'I said I was doing work experience for a few days, but I went along and filmed all these people in trees and charging cranes [instead].'

Will got well and truly busted though. When he returned to college, his housemaster strolled into his dorm ... only to see Will on TV surrounded by angry protesters, who were burning a crane. It wasn't quite the work experience his teacher had had in mind.

But despite the odd hitch, Will's dedication and studious ways eventually paid off, and he left sixth-form college with two As and a B in Politics, Ancient History and English. These impressive new qualifications won him a place at the prestigious Exeter University. Will was delighted.

Shortly before he started his university studies, however, an incident took place that Will regrets to this day. Aged nineteen, he went out drinking with some friends in Oxford one night. When the evening came to a close, Will decided to drive himself home – even though he'd had a few drinks. When he got there, safely and in one piece, he felt that all-too-familiar, slightly drunken urge to go for a kebab. But instead of walking the short distance from his home to the kebab shop, he foolishly jumped into his car again – and found himself going the wrong way down a one-way system. It was only then that he spotted the police car.

The police, naturally, followed him home. They quickly realized that Will was tipsy (he agrees that tripping up in front of them probably wasn't the best move), so they took him to the local police station where he was charged.

Later that summer, though, things went from bad to worse. Will mistakenly missed his court hearing, and when Robin took his worried son down to the police station to explain his no-show, Will was fitted with handcuffs and taken to a cell. Eventually, he was given a fine and banned from driving for a year and half. Will still feels terrible about the episode, and is deeply regretful. He is keen to learn from his mistake. 'Looking back it was a good lesson for me to learn,' he says. 'I was extremely lucky not to have hurt anyone else or myself, and drinking and driving is a totally irresponsible thing to do.'

Come October, Will managed to put the incident behind him and began his degree course at Exeter. Having already done an A Level in politics, which he had found fascinating, Will decided to continue with the subject because, 'I felt I should know about what was going on in my country.'

He was a hugely popular student, and was lusted after by what a friend conservatively describes as 'half the female student population'. He regularly showed off his quirky sense of humour, and once turned up to a university formal ball dressed as a cheetah. He also became well known for wearing tank tops to lectures, and for his collection of hats, which he refers to as his 'tea cosies'.

Will quickly became involved in a number of extra-curricular activities. During his third year he organized a charity ball, which raised £20,000 for an HIV and AIDS charity called Positive Action South West. He also made a short film, a mockumentary called *University of Life*, and, as was to be expected with his passion for performing, joined a theatre group called Footlights. Will was thrilled when he landed the lead role of Curly in the group's production of *Oklahoma!* 'I really enjoyed it and doing that gave me a lot of confidence,' he says of the show.

But, as his friend Katie Russel, the musical's producer,

reveals, the show didn't always run smoothly, and they did experience the occasional hitch. 'I remember one night the curtain went up, the music started and the spotlight lit up an empty stage. There was no Will,' Katie recalls. 'We were in such a panic frantically trying to find him. In the end we found him backstage just pottering around, not aware of the time. I could have killed him.'

And Will has his own memory of a faux pas. 'I was supposed to be playing this really tough guy and the whole scene was based around me firing this toy gun. Anyway, the gun didn't go off, so the whole show ended up in chaos, because nothing that followed made sense. We ad-libbed for about five minutes and it was hilarious.'

As for most people, Will's university days weren't simply centred on the studying, or even on the many extra-curricular activities available to him. There was also a certain amount of socializing to be done. And although Will wasn't the kind of student who spent *every* night drinking cheap pints in the student union, he does admit to being a pretty impressive boozer. 'We used to go to this pub opposite a bakery, and we used to call an all-day session a Princess Leia, and pop over the road and get a couple of Danish pastries to stick to the sides of our heads,' he reminisces fondly. But he continues: 'I had been out on one of these all-day sessions and I tried to walk home late at night, and I fell flat on my face and cut my head. I had blood all over me. It was like I'd walked off a horror film set.'

Dangerous drinking sessions aside, Will also made time to keep up his primary passion: music. Already a keen singer, Will found the perfect places to practise during his time in the historical Devonshire city. 'I used to sing in this car park in Exeter because the sound was so great. It had great acoustics. I used to go there when I was pissed off. It was a release for me,' he reveals. 'But most of the time I'd go to this little chapel near my university and sing away, because it's also got great acoustics. I'd just sing whatever I felt like, but not on a Sunday morning as I didn't think they'd appreciate it!'

It was while he was studying at university that Will's first major TV appearance came about. He was bunking off with a hangover one day back in 1999, watching every student's favourite TV show, *This Morning*, when he heard the presenters Richard and Judy talking about a boy-band competition that the programme was running. Could fate already be playing a hand in his future? He swiftly dispatched an audition tape and sat back and waited.

Soon, he received a letter informing him that he'd made it to the last seventy-five competitors and was summoned to London for off-camera auditions.

The seventy-five aspiring boy-banders were then cut down to nine, and each was given a mini-audition live on the show in front of a panel of judges, which included a certain TV presenter called Kate Thornton, and a record-company executive called Simon Cowell. Music exec Simon had kicked off his career at EMI Records in 1979, and went on to work in A&R at BMG. He was a big cheese in the music industry, working behind the scenes to find acts that would take the commercial music scene by storm. As his duties included signing new bands, he was constantly on the lookout for new talent. When Will first encountered him, his successes included Robson and Jerome, Sonia, boy band 5ive, Zig & Zag and that classic 1997 Christmas number one from the Teletubbies, 'Teletubbies Say Eh-Oh'. Unbeknown to Will, both Simon and Kate would come to play a big part in his life a little further down the line.

A jubilant Will made it down to the final four in the competition, alongside another soon-to-be familiar face: Lee

Ryan from boy band Blue. Simon Cowell said of the lucky winners, 'We've tried to find people with star quality and these guys can sing and dance.'

But Will wasn't totally happy with his first brush with fame. 'We went for a makeover and they made me look like a monkey. They brushed down my fringe. Eurgh!' he laughs.

Sadly, though, the band didn't take off – in Will's words the band just 'didn't happen' – but the experience did give him a taste of the music business. He decided there and then that a career in singing was something he definitely wanted to pursue.

Will has always had a passion for music. He loves everything from classical to pop, with his favourite song of all time being Joan Armatrading's 'Love And Affection'. As he is also passionate about other forms of expression, such as art, photography and writing, it was almost inevitable that he would end up doing something creative with his life. While politics was fascinating to him, the pull of the stage was to prove too strong – he knew that he would never be happy simply doing a stuffy office job.

After his experience on *This Morning*, Will headed back to university with his aspirations to be a singer foremost in his mind, and resigned himself to the fact that his studies might suffer due to his new choice of direction. However, his lecturers proved to be incredibly supportive, especially as Will was always upfront about his musical aspirations. 'If he missed class it was because of his music. He never lied about it,' says his personal tutor and politics teacher Dr Larbi Sadiki. 'We understood and gave him a bit of leeway.'

Another of his tutors even wrote Will a glowing reference when he travelled to London's Guild Hall to audition as a jazz musician. But sadly things didn't go quite according to plan: Will discovered that he'd turned up for the audition on the wrong day, and had to head back to Devon disappointed.

As for his fellow students, it appears that they could see the potential in Will even before he started to get real recognition for his talents. 'I remember some of the students saying before classes, "This guy's going to be a star,"' reveals Dr Larbi. In fact, it was one of Will's classmates who alerted him to the advert for *Pop Idol* in the *News of the World*, just days before they were due to graduate. Never one to back away from a challenge, Will called the number on the advert and heard the dulcet tones of Capital FM DJ 'Dr Fox' on the other end of the line, telling him all about the upcoming *Pop Idol* contest. Will quickly went on to the internet, printed out the application form and filled it in. He later quipped that it took him longer to complete than his final exams, but it certainly proved to be worth his time.

He eventually posted off the application on 28 June 2001, and then he sat back and waited. And waited.

Day after day Will excitedly anticipated the post, but he became increasingly disillusioned when he didn't receive a reply, so he decided to go to plan B. He got himself a job as a waiter to pay the bills, and also secured a place at a performing arts college called the Arts Educational School, based in Chiswick, London. 'When I left university I thought, "I want to go and sing," but I didn't want to be that naive person without any training,' he explains.

Just as he was preparing his move to London, however, the *Pop Idol* reply he had been waiting for dropped through his letterbox on Tuesday 7 August, inviting him to audition in London on 5 September. Making sure he wrote down the correct date in his diary (he wasn't going to make *that* mistake again), Will set about planning his audition piece and put in plenty of practise.

Proving the old adage that buses always come at once, around this time Will was also offered a full-time job. He had done work experience at Sony Records during his time at university, to gain some insight into the music industry, and they were keen to snap him up. But his heart was set on working on stage rather than behind the scenes, so after much deliberation he turned them down. 'Earning money is at the forefront of people's minds [when they graduate]. There was a job I could have done at Sony. I would not have had to worry. Instead, I took out another loan. I wanted to go for what I really wanted to do,' he says of his decision.

But before his audition there was the small matter of Will's graduation ceremony: he graduated with a high 2:2 in politics from Exeter. His tutors had expected him to attain a 2:1, but his musical ambitions had caused him to sway from the academic path somewhat. It was just after he graduated that Will's dad Robin decided to have a serious chat with him about his future. 'I did the fatherly "get a proper job" thing, and advised him against following a singing career. I thought I'd persuaded him and suggested he get a normal job and continue singing in the evenings,' says Robin. 'But he sensibly ignored me, and the next thing I knew he had a place at a performing arts college in London. I'm so glad he went against my advice.'

It was because of this family reticence that Will initially decided not to tell his relatives about his *Pop Idol* audition. He confided in some friends, but he wanted to keep the whole thing under wraps, until he knew whether or not anything would come of it.

In himself, Will felt ready to face the huge challenge ahead. He knew that he had learned a lot at university, which would stand him in good stead for any potential knock-backs – should they come. 'I've been to university, which is a soul-searching time, and I came out a stronger person. I have strong principles and opinions and I stick to them,' he says.

Little did he know it then, but this individuality and self-esteem were to prove priceless in the upcoming contest. For Will, there was never a moment to look back from this point on.

CHAPTER TWO

Audition Hell

Over 10,000 people completed application forms for the first series of *Pop Idol*. Auditions were held in Manchester, London and Glasgow over a four-week period. The competition was never going to be an easy ride.

It was up to the judges – DJ and TV presenter 'Dr' Neil Fox; Nicki Chapman, a creative director from 19 Management; pop guru and record producer Pete Waterman; and, of course, sharp-tongued record-company executive Simon Cowell – to discover the future of British music. And they had quite a job on their hands. Audition performances ranged from the brilliant to the bizarre – from fancy-dress costumes to tiny bikinis – and boasted the likes of 'cuddly' Rik Waller, curly-haired firecracker Zoe Birkett, plus some chap called Darius Danesh.

Pop Idol bosses got their first glimpse of Will during the auditions at the ExCel conference centre in London's Docklands, in September 2001.

Before he was even allowed in to see the frightening foursome, though, he had to convince the show's assistant producer, Claire Howell, that he was good enough to enter the hallowed audition room where the judges resided, by showcasing his audition piece.

'I have to tell you, it didn't go well at the beginning,' Will says of his performance of the Aretha Franklin classic 'Until You Come Back To Me', 'but just as I got to the rifty bit I think I managed to pull it back.'

Thankfully Claire agreed, and he was asked to return two days later, when he auditioned for the producer – who was also suitably impressed. Will was definitely through to the next stage: he would finally get his moment of glory (and fear) in front of Simon, Nicki, Pete and Foxy.

But he had quite a wait on his hands. In fact, Will was the very last person to be seen by the judges in the entire competition. He admits that due to that added pressure, and thanks to the countless TV cameras, which were recording his every move, he was nervous as hell. '[The TV cameras] were being thrust in our faces just as we were about to walk through the door and audition. I really wanted to concentrate on the singing, not being on a TV show,' he complains.

What followed was a bizarre rendition of the Jackson 5's 'Blame It On The Boogie' … accompanied by a weird lolloping dance. It didn't impress a stern-faced Simon, who also failed to recognize Will from their previous meeting on *This Morning*. However, he later joked, 'It wasn't until the other day that I realized I had seen Will perform before. If I had known we'd meet in years to come I'd have been a lot nicer to him first time round!'

To make matters worse, Will's laid-back sense of style (he wore his granddad's jumper to the audition) got him noticed for all the wrong reasons. 'You're wearing a pair of old jeans, shoes that have never seen a polish in their life, a top that's seen better days and shirt that's got an egg stain on it. You think I'm going to put you through? No way, kid,' moaned Pete.

However, luckily some of the other judges could see that if you scratched the dodgy-looking surface, there was plenty of talent nestling underneath that rough exterior. Despite the bad dance moves and grubby clothes, Will's voice shone through. While Foxy called him cheesy (pot, kettle, anyone?) and Nicki said she didn't like his dancing, a bemused Simon still told him somewhat reluctantly, 'Okay, we'll see you through to the next round.'

Looking back, Will says that he is embarrassed by the audition, but he's also happy that he had the guts to go through with it in the first place. 'I cringe at my first audition, but I'm still kind of proud of it. Just for walking in that room if nothing else. That was so scary.'

The lucky one hundred who had made it through the demanding first stages were invited to perform at the Criterion Theatre in London's Piccadilly, where they were to be whittled down to the final fifty. Will had spent the days before practising his singing and dancing and, importantly, making sure he had something decent to wear. Things were getting serious and the competition was tough. So were the judges. 'We've seen some really good people. We've also seen some people who have slipped through the net,' admitted Nicki of the final selection.

And she wasn't wrong. The judges had no problem whatsoever in cutting twenty-four people almost instantly, thanks to screeching renditions of popular hits from the kinds of singers who would be booed off a karaoke competition, let alone a nationwide talent search.

Needless to say, Will made it through after wowing the judges with his performance of American boy band O-Town's hit, 'All Or Nothing'.

The seventy-six remaining rivals were then split into groups of three. While the girls had to sing Aretha Franklin's 'Say A Little Prayer', the boys were given The Drifters' 'Up On The Roof' to contend with.

It was after these performances, when the contestants were sitting around waiting to hear the results of their latest auditions, that Will switched on a TV for the first time that day, and heard about the two planes which had crashed into the Twin Towers in New York. 'I felt sick and the auditions suddenly seemed utterly trivial and meaningless,' he recalls.

He headed straight to his friend Mary's house in west London – a destination which was soon to become his new home – to watch the coverage on TV, before making his way back to the theatre to hear the judges' decisions.

At 9.30 p.m., three hours after everyone was due to discover who had made it through to the next stage, the auditionees were divided into four groups, then escorted to separate rooms by one of the show's producers. But the pain of waiting wasn't over, and there was yet more of a delay before Simon Cowell finally entered Will's room to tell the anxious potential pop idols their fate.

'We've been backwards and forwards and had to make some difficult decisions tonight, I'm afraid,' he told them, before adding, 'However, you should be pleased to know that you are through to the next round.'

In the midst of the excitement, a grinning and rather dumbstruck Will shed a few tears, and contemplated the fact that he had made it through to the final stages.

But his initial joy soon turned to concern after his group were told that they were considered the 'maybe' contestants, and had only just escaped being unceremoniously cut. 'I was in the "maybe" room,' recalls Will. 'We had to wait three-and-a-half hours. We heard two rooms cheering and I was thinking, "There's no way I'm through." Then Simon came in and said, "I'm sorry … to keep you waiting." I just thought, "You're evil!" and I burst into tears.'

There was another shock to come, though, when the

contestants were told that eleven more people would be dismissed the following day. The experience was becoming increasingly stressful, and after yet more auditions, during which Will sang George Michael's 'Fast Love', the contenders were gathered together once again, this time for the final showdown: the final judges' cut. After this stage of the competition, the cull of singers would be left in the hands of the public. Said a happy Nicki, 'I do have my Pop Idol in front of us, which is a very pleasing thought.'

And then it was time to discover which final fifty would be hitting the live show … Will Young, alias contestant 6691, was one of the lucky ones, securing his place in the last fifty after that series of nail-biting auditions. But his family were still in the dark about his remarkable achievement. It was only when the auditions were scheduled to be shown on TV – and Will was forced to come clean about his involvement with the programme – that his family were alerted to his participation. 'We had no idea he was even on the show until he mentioned it,' recalls Will's brother, Rupert. 'Then we switched on an episode when the judges were deciding who should be in the final fifty – and there he was. But that was so typical of him.'

The boys' dad Robin agrees. 'He didn't want to tell us until he knew he had a real chance of winning. We were completely surprised because we had no idea he could sing that well. That's William all over; he does his own thing and then you find out about it. He's a very determined chap. The only time we saw him sing was in a musical at university, as Curly in *Oklahoma!* But singing "Oh, What A Beautiful Morning" isn't quite what he's doing now.'

At last, the problem of how to tell his family he had entered *Pop Idol* had been solved, but Will's success at the auditions left him with another dilemma. By now he had started his first term at Arts Ed college, and he wasn't supposed to go for any auditions while at the school. Although, strictly speaking, his auditions for *Pop Idol* had taken place before he'd even walked through the gates, his continued participation in the show meant that he would have to take four days off from classes for voice and dance coaching. He was left with no choice but to confess. Will also felt it would be better for him to be upfront with his tutors, rather than for them to find out when they turned on their televisions one Saturday night, only to spot a familiar face singing his heart out onscreen.

Ultimately, however, Will decided that it would be best if he left the college altogether, so that he could fully concentrate his attentions on *Pop Idol*. Even though he had loved his time at Arts Ed and learnt a lot, he felt that he would be doing such a prestigious school an injustice if he was unable to attend all his classes. Moreover, being involved in *Pop Idol* had made him realize something about his future in music. 'As soon as I was in the last fifty, I realized that musical theatre wasn't for me,' he says candidly.

Despite Will's turnabout on his studies, his former Arts Ed headmaster, Ian Watt-Smith, isn't bitter about his erstwhile student's early departure, and is in fact overjoyed about Will's success. 'I am absolutely thrilled. He is a delightful bloke – a smashing guy, intelligent, sensitive, sophisticated and so versatile. In his end-of-term project he played an Australian Aboriginal in *Our Country's Good*. He was covered in body paint and gave a wonderfully dignified performance,' Watt-Smith revealed. 'I am sorry that he's no longer with us because he was such a positive influence – so clear-headed and mature.

'I see Will very much as "the complete performer", even though he was only with us for one term. He acknowledged that he had learned so much in terms of presentation. He is a genuine all-rounder, but he has decided he wants to sing on his own rather than appear in shows, so I think he has made the right decision for him.'

Back in the tense world of *Pop Idol*, Will's next audition date was named. He was to be one of ten contenders battling it out in the fourth heat of the TV shows, for which he started rehearsals in November 2001. In the weeks leading up to his audition, he kept a keen eye on how his competitors were doing by watching the programme each Saturday night, to see who got through to the next round. It was important for him to know who he would be up against, should he be lucky enough to make it to the final ten.

As the day of his TV appearance loomed, Will joined the other nine contestants from his heat at Teddington Studios, for vocal training and styling. Renowned vocal coaches David and Carrie Grant and musical arranger Mike Dixon helped him with the arrangement for his choice of song, The Doors' 'Light My Fire', while three dress rehearsals helped to calm his nerves for the following day's filming.

But then something happened that threw Will completely, and his mind was immediately taken off the competition.

With just a day to go before Will took to the stage, a very close family friend, Will's dad's PA, Karen, passed away. Will was extremely close to her and felt the loss deeply. 'If I had phoned her and said, "I've lost my head," she'd have said in her wonderful Scottish accent, "Okay, Will, don't panic. Stay where you are and I'll find it for you." Such a wonderful lady cruelly taken away from us by a brain tumour – she didn't deserve to go.

'She was a very important person for all of us – she was a wonderful woman who would listen to any problem anyone had and talk them through it. She had a great attitude and helped all of us at different times. She was part of the family. She would always tell you the truth as well, no matter if you didn't want to hear it. Her passing came so quickly and it affected me badly. It was kind of a turning point for me ... Until then, I'd been shy and quiet, but her death made me realize you should focus on the positive. She influenced me a lot in the way I approached the contest towards the end. I changed for the better.'

At last the big day came and it was Will's turn to sing for the public's vote. It soon became clear that the intensive classes he had taken at Arts Ed, together with the training he had done with David and Carrie, had stood him in good stead for his first real *Pop Idol* performance.

But things didn't run completely smoothly. Despite being one of the quieter contestants, who spent much of his time backstage writing his diary, while others were larking about together in the Green Room, Will showed that he wasn't as meek as some people first thought.

After delivering a show-stopping performance, which showcased his effortless talent and originality, Will was praised by most of the judges for his confident debut performance. Simon Cowell, however, had another opinion. Criticizing Will's efforts, he said, 'Distinctly average. I just thought it was totally normal. In the context of the show I honestly don't think it will be good enough.'

Will, who had become increasingly angry about Simon's consistently negative comments as he watched the show week after week, hit back by (very politely) saying, 'I think it's nice that you've given opinions in this show. In previous shows you haven't. You've just projected insults and it's been terrible to watch. It is your opinion but I don't agree with it. I don't think it was average. I don't think you could ever call that average, but it is your opinion and I respect that, so thank you very much.'

Afterwards Will joked to the show's hosts Ant and Dec by way of explanation: 'I know my dad would be sitting there going, "You're not taking that, my boy. Annabel, get the shotgun!"'

And Will was right. His dad Robin was totally in favour of his outburst. 'It was a very proud moment for me. I thought William handled it wonderfully – he was polite as usual but made Simon apologize. We thought Simon was unfair and quite clearly wrong. He said William's song was average, but we thought it was anything but.'

Later, when Will was asked what his proudest moment of the entire competition was, he replied, 'It was during the heats, when I spoke my mind to Simon. That was good. I suppose I was lucky because I've been trained to disagree with people in a polite way, having done politics at university. I think I was surprised how it came out because I forgot what I said until I watched it back, and then I was like, "Ooh, yes! I like that!"

'I remember talking to my dad before going on and him saying to me, "I didn't bring you up to take rudeness." I don't think the judges were particularly rude to me, but I just went in all guns blazing anyway. I was so surprised by what that brought out in me. It made me realize that I had strength and determination. It was quite liberating.'

With the show having been pre-recorded on a Wednesday, Will and his fellow *Pop Idol* contestants had to wait until the show was screened on Saturday to learn the outcome of the viewers' vote. And Will soon discovered that his bravery in standing up to Simon – along with his brilliant first performance – had paid off. When the results were announced it was revealed that Will had romped to victory, winning an incredible 41.5 per cent of the overall vote. Needless to say he was on cloud nine, and he and a group of friends celebrated his win by going clubbing until the early hours.

But there's no rest for the wicked, and in no time Will had to start rehearsals for his next TV performance. This time round he chose to sing his first audition song, Aretha Franklin's 'Until You Come Back To Me', and he got busy practising his rendition. The first show to feature the final ten was going to be totally live, so the pressure was well and truly on.

As was fast becoming a bit of a habit, Will pulled it off magnificently, and the judges were quick to praise him after his belting performance of the soul classic.

'I think you've got the most unique voice I've heard in twenty years. You're fantastic. You do songs your own way,' raved Pete, while Nicki gushed, 'You could be a singer from any era.' And although Dr Fox had a few unkind words to say about Will's jumper (would Will ever get his 'look' right?), the DJ couldn't help but agree that he was brilliant.

But what of Simon? 'William, first question, has your dad got his shotgun with him?' the record-company executive quipped, before adding, 'I have to say, William, you, more than anyone, you've humbled me from last time. I watched your performance back and realized I'd made a huge mistake with what I said, and I thought the way you handled yourself was with dignity. The public voted against Big Mouth, and I'm delighted for you.'

A smiling Will replied graciously, 'That means a lot to me, Simon.'

With the final fifty now down to the final ten, the competition was hotting up. One contestant was to be voted off each week, until only two remained for the final sing-off, which would decide who the nation's Pop Idol would be. It was serious stuff.

Will admits that when he made it to the final ten, he finally felt that he might truly have a chance of winning. He said, 'I don't think you would enter a competition like this unless you thought you could win it. But there's a difference between proving you can win it and thinking you can win it.'

As the prize edged closer, the financial repercussions of winning the show also figured in Will's mind. Although he didn't enter *Pop Idol* for the money, he admitted that a few extra pounds wouldn't go amiss, and it was the kind of perk that anyone would be more than happy to have. 'You don't want to start doing some competition thinking of the money at the end of it, you want to sing,' explained Will. 'I'm terrible with money – I have £9,000 of debt with student loans and overdrafts. Money doesn't drive me in the slightest. But it would be nice to have some.'

Up until this point, Will had been living happily with his friend Mary in her west London flat. Now there were only ten contestants left, however, the *Pop Idol* producers arranged for the remaining competitors to move into the Marriott Hotel in Maida Vale together, so they could get to know each other better and help each other through the strange experience of starring in a top TV show.

The other aspiring stars who had made it to the final ten were a hotbed of talent, from the sweet and soulful to the fun and pop. But they all had one thing in common – a shared love of all things musical. They were to become Will's pseudo-family for the next nine nail-biting weeks.

Sixteen-year-old Zoe Birkett from County Durham turned everyone's heads with her amazing curly hair, huge smile and belting voice. Her performance of Whitney Houston's 'One Moment In Time' got Zoe through to the final ten, and from the very start she was singled out as 'one to watch'. With a talent that belied her years, she still remained a fun-loving girl at heart, and she and fellow youngster Gareth Gates soon bonded.

Like Zoe, seventeen-year-old Bradford boy Gareth Gates was an instant hit with the judges, thanks to his boy-next-door good looks and cheeky grin. His stutter also got him noticed during the first round of auditions, so from the very beginning of the TV show he was one of the few contestants to be remembered nationwide. Everyone was amazed at his ability to sing perfectly in spite of his stutter, and his determination to make it as a singer – regardless of his speaking skills – melted the hearts of teenage girls and grannies everywhere. Gareth's spiky hair later became a huge talking point, but he admitted during the show: 'Up until the age of twelve, it was a bowl cut. Then after that I had "curtains" for ages.' He landed a place in the final ten by singing 'Flying Without Wings' by boy band Westlife, a song that practically became his signature track in the competition.

Because of the massive exposure Gareth had had from the start of the show, Will was aware that the young singer was a hot contender for the *Pop Idol* crown. Despite his front-running status, though, Gareth was just as astonished as the rest of the final ten at the interest being shown in them by the press. It was a journey they were all making together.

Another finalist was twenty-five-year-old brunette Hayley Evetts, from Birmingham, who was told by a smitten Simon Cowell, 'You're so sexy!', during her bid to make it to the final ten. She had aspired to be a nurse, but her passion for performing led her to *Pop Idol*. She and Will instantly hit it off, but it was her friendship with younger man Gareth that later fuelled the gossip pages of the tabloids, when it was rumoured that she had dated the teenager for a short time during the competition. Neither of them has ever admitted to being more than friends, however. It was her rendition of 'I Have Nothing' by Whitney Houston that got her voted into the final ten.

Down-to-earth, twenty-six-year-old, father-of-one Aaron Bayley hailed from Newcastle, and swiftly became good mates with everyone on the show. The popular train driver with the cheery smile already had no doubts about what he would spend his money on if he made a million off the back of the show. 'My girlfriend would probably want a boob job,' he said. 'I'd want an executive suite at St James's Park and a Lamborghini Diablo.' He warbled 'Walking In Memphis' by Mark Cohn to win his place in the all-important final ten.

Pretty, smiley Jessica Garlick, meanwhile, soon became known for her straight-talking ways. The twenty-year-old from South Wales admitted that even at school she was considered to be outspoken, and her reports reflected this. 'Every one of them said I was confident. Quite bossy, actually. They'd say, "Jessica is a born leader,"' she revealed. She sang her way into the final ten thanks to Madonna's 'Crazy For You', a song she'd also picked for her initial audition with the judges; a performance which had made Pete Waterman cry. It was certainly second time lucky for Jessica.

The seventh contestant to make it through was 'cuddly' twenty-year-old Rik Waller, from Rainham in Kent, who had enjoyed almost as much press coverage as Gareth in the show's opening weeks, though for very different reasons. 'I Can't Make You Love Me' by George Michael proved to be Rik's winning song, putting him through to the final ten. Thirty-stone Rik admitted that his school reports had always labelled him 'lazy', but he had enough get up and go to enter *Pop Idol*, and although his look was anything but that of a stereotypical pop star, he impressed everyone with his amazing vocal talent. Just as the climactic live shows featuring the final ten started, however, he sadly had to drop out of the competition due to a throat infection.

Instead, twenty-one-year-old Darius Danesh from Glasgow was drafted in to take over Rik's place. Strapping and surprisingly sexy, the Scottish singer was dubbed the 'comeback kid' after he defied the odds to land a place in the final ten. Darius was already something of a celebrity, having humiliated himself on *Pop Stars* earlier in the year with his now-infamous 'alternative' interpretation of Britney Spears's 'Baby One More Time', but he came back to prove what he was made of on *Pop Idol*, and luckily fate was on his side this time round. When Rik bowed out due to illness, Darius was invited to take his place, being the contestant from Rik's heat with the third-highest public vote. Immediately, he settled in, and the *Pop Idol* family had a brand new member ensconced.

There were three more lucky singers competing alongside Will and the others for the *Pop Idol* crown. Sweet-natured Laura Doherty from Northern Ireland had already tried her hand at TV presenting before landing a place on the show. The gorgeous curly-haired nineteen-year-old had a lucky charm in the shape of her boyfriend's ring, which she wore throughout the competition. 'He had no choice in the matter. I took it off him to wear!' she confessed. 'Tears In Heaven' by Eric Clapton earned her a place in the final ten.

Meanwhile, chiselled Korben from Bedford belted out 'From The Heart' by Another Level to make it to the show's finals. He was confident that he had the elusive 'star quality' the judges were looking for, saying that his teachers had recognized his talent while he was still at school. The handsome twenty-one-year-old was open about being gay, but later told a newspaper that he felt this might have hindered his chances of winning.

Finally, pretty, blonde-haired, eighteen-year-old Rosie Ribbons, from South Wales, completed the set. She became a firm favourite of Pete Waterman's, who promised to make her a star. But that of course was the whole point of the competition – and the other contestants were just as keen to secure success. Despite the fact that they were supposed rivals, however, none of the singers let the competition affect their burgeoning friendships. Luckily, they all got on fantastically, and Will was to find the group a huge support as the show progressed.

Although they weren't about to start earning fortunes this early on, one thing Will was pleased about was the fact that all the contestants got expenses for appearing on *Pop Idol* – but he was hardly being lavish with the handout. 'We get expenses but the thing is, I haven't spent any money,' he admitted at the time. 'The only money I spend is on Saturday night if I go out with my friends after the show. So at least my overdraft's gone down a bit.'

The first week with the final ten contestants was a nervous time for all the singers, especially when they heard the news that Rik Waller had left the competition for good due to his continuing throat infection. The whole episode made the other contestants feel a bit anxious.

This first week immediately gave the contestants a taste of what life might be like if they were to win the show, as they undertook their first piece of PR. The talented ten were invited to go on the popular show *This Morning*, which gave Will an odd feeling of stepping back in time. 'I had the strangest déjà vu – it's where we did that boy-band competition all those years ago,' he said.

Meanwhile, the contenders decided to buy each other little Christmas gifts, which proved to be an excellent bonding experience. Will gave Aaron some Elvis socks, while Hayley bought Will a hat and two toy cars – because his car had been towed away the previous week. But with the jollity over, it was time to get down to business: the singing competition.

When it came to the performances in the first week of the final heats, Laura was in tears after being told by Pete that she wasn't a great singer, but Will's rendition of Aretha Franklin's 'Until You Come Back To Me' earned him 27.3 per cent of the votes. Bradford boy Gareth Gates was hot on his tail with 26.3 per cent, but as the contestants weren't told the specifics of the poll, each remained in the dark about their individual popularity. None of them knew who was in the lead at this early stage – an ignorance that would continue right up to the final show.

The first progamme's casualty was Korben, and the reality of his departure hit everyone hard. With a mere eight weeks to go before the final sing-off, it was time for everyone to raise their game if they wanted to be crowned the *Pop Idol* king or queen.

Week two proved to be every bit as nerve-racking, as it was time to cut yet another contestant from the competition. The group were beginning to realize that this was going to be one tough show. The theme was Christmas songs, and while Rosie didn't impress with her rendition of 'Santa Baby', Aaron's 'Blue Christmas' went down a storm with the older members of the audience.

Will, meanwhile, managed to make 'Walking In A Winter Wonderland' his own by doing a slowed-down version. 'I love that song. I've decided to slow it down but seriously jazz it up. I can't wait to perform it,' Will said before the show. However, as ever his style choices were under the spotlight: his saucy see-through shirt didn't impress the judges.

At the end of the night it was three ladies – Jessica, Rosie and Laura – who found themselves sitting next to Ant and Dec on the 'sofa of doom', waiting to hear which one of them would be going home. Sadly, it was a tearful Jessica who had to say goodbye, but she admitted: 'This has been the best experience of my life.'

For Will, however, the experience was just beginning. For the second week running he topped the viewers' votes, with 22.6 per cent, with Gareth and new boy Darius breathing heavily down his neck with 20.8 per cent and 19 per cent of the vote respectively. It seemed the lad from Hungerford was really getting into his stride.

In the lead-up to the third round of the finals, the gang got to do a shoot with *OK!* magazine – and Rosie found herself wearing a pair of trousers that cost an incredible £2,000. For at least one of the group, such a thing would soon be a common occurrence. But Will admitted that he didn't really enjoy the shoot – no matter how exciting it seemed. 'To be honest I wasn't in the mood,' he said at the time. For Will, the exhilarating part of the show was the music, and the third week offered the potential for some really challenging songs, as the remaining aspiring idols belted out timeless tracks written by the legendary crooner Burt Bacharach.

Having been in danger of being booted out the last couple of weeks, Laura got a huge boost when she was praised for her performance of Sandie Shaw's 'Always Something There To Remind Me'. Will also received some great feedback from the judges for his performance of 'Wives And Lovers', when Pete told him: 'The bad news is you're not a Pop Idol. The good news is you're a superstar.'

But it seemed Laura's improved performance didn't manage to warm the viewers' hearts. Achieving one of the lowest voting scores that week, along with Rosie and Aaron, it was inevitable that one of them would leave. Everyone was gutted when it was announced that friendly Aaron would be heading home to Newcastle. He had played a key part in the group dynamic, in that he'd helped to keep spirits up week after week, and everyone knew he would be sorely missed. 'Losing Aaron is a real shame because the group will suffer for him leaving,' admitted Will. But there was no time to dwell on people exiting the show – yet again Will was riding high with the highest votes from viewers, but now only 0.3 per cent separated him from teenage warbler Gareth Gates, whose increasingly professional performances were garnering him more and more votes as each week passed.

Come week four of the final shows, the crowds outside the studio had grown – and so had the tension inside. But Will wasn't short of praise from the judges during these all-important weeks. After an incredible performance of Bill Withers' 'Ain't No Sunshine', Nicki told him, 'You always pick the right song for you when you perform, and when we talk about the Pop Idol or the person to entertain us it's the whole package – not just about the voice, it's everything – and you really do deliver. We're paying you compliments and I don't think it's going to your head. You're still going to remain the same, Will, so keep going, because you're getting it right!'

Nicki was spot on with her observation. Talent aside, one of the things that the audience liked most about Will was his ability to stay down to earth, despite all the attention he was receiving. Also, even if he made the odd mistake, Will managed to smile through it and continue like a true professional. These characteristics, when coupled with his unique voice, made for an impressive whole. Will's bid for a singing career seemed to be going to plan. Meanwhile, that same week Pete told him, 'You sing the song equally as good as Bill Withers does. That's your sort of song.' And it seemed the viewers agreed, when Will snaffled a fabulous 29.9 per cent of the vote. Gareth trailed him with 23.3 per cent, but it was a teary Laura who eventually said her goodbyes. 'I'm going to miss being in the show but when it's all over I can hold my head up high,' she sniffed proudly.

At this time, although *Pop Idol* was growing in popularity each week and the media exposure of the contestants was even becoming a little extreme, Will was still trying to live his life the same way he had always done. The realization that he was soon to be very famous hadn't yet kicked in. But one Sunday afternoon, as he sat in the pub with his mates, he had his first taste of recognition. 'I did get recognized, but you know what? It was alright. It wasn't bad. I had a few people come up to me, but they all said nice things. I think that's the good thing about the show – people are so involved in it,' he remarked.

By now, of course, *Pop Idol* was one of the highest-rating programmes on TV – it was a bona fide water-cooler show. And, whether Will realized it or not, the programme had made him a star. As well as the *OK!* magazine photo shoot, he was doing interviews with leading publications such as *Heat* and *Smash Hits*, and his face was becoming increasingly well known. In fact, as the show went on Will started to be recognized regularly (which, he concedes, was sometimes down to the TV cameras which followed him pretty much everywhere), and he was getting used to signing autographs and posing for pictures with his ever-increasing legion of fans.

But he was always careful to make sure that he didn't let any of it go to his head, even when, in the run-up to week five, the finalists were whisked off to Hanbury Manor Health Farm. Here they were put through their dance paces by respected choreographer Paul Roberts. Will and Zoe were considered to be getting on best with the complicated routines, Hayley held her own, while Darius, Rosie and Gareth all found the sessions a touch daunting. Will was delighted to be told by Paul that he was the best dancer out of the boys – and it was praise that had to see him through that week's show, which proved to be a bit of a disaster for all the contestants.

It was Abba week on *Pop Idol*, and even Pete acknowledged that Abba songs are hard to sing. Will revealed that he only chose his track, 'The Name Of The Game', because he 'couldn't get to grips with any of the others'. Rosie, Hayley and Darius didn't get great feedback from the judges, but they remained impressed by Will and Zoe's renditions.

That week, it was time for Rosie to pack her bags. She found herself up against Darius and Hayley in the final three. Pete cheered her up no end, though, when he announced: 'She could be a superstar.' But there were bad tidings for Will. Although he had been leading each week so far, by the end of week five Will had been overtaken by Gareth, who was the very clear winner that week with 36.6 per cent of the vote to Will's 25.2 per cent. This proved that it was still anybody's competition. All the contestants were going to have to work extremely hard to win the show – nobody, by any stretch of the imagination, had it in the bag.

The remaining contestants now moved into an apartment together at the top of the Marriott Hotel, where they helped each other deal with the increasing pressure of the competition. By now they all got on like a house on fire and would take turns with household chores. Though they divided up chef duty, too, it was often Darius who would whip them up a feast each night. 'He is a very good cook. He takes it very seriously,' Will revealed.

Everyone found week six – the big-band week – especially tough. With just five contestants left, they were feeling the strain more than ever. But in the days running up to the show they got plenty of help from voice coaches Carrie and David Grant, and also got to see some friendly faces when they all headed back to their home towns for a meet and greet with fans.

It wasn't the first time Will had returned home since the competition had really got going. Keen to avoid becoming a diva or a self-obsessed celebrity, he had been making regular trips back home to see his family in Berkshire, as well as visiting his uni mates in Exeter, to escape from the *Pop Idol* madness and keep his feet on the ground.

Nevertheless, that didn't mean that he didn't allow himself to be a bit 'showbiz' every now and again, and enjoy his taste of the high life. And week six saw him relish one of the most memorable moments from his whole *Pop Idol* experience: his first film premiere in January 2002. Along with the other remaining contestants – Zoe, Gareth, Darius and Hayley – he attended the *Black Hawk Down* celebrity screening in London's Leicester Square.

Looking dapper in a simple smart black suit and white shirt, and with the girls in glam designer dresses, Will and the other excited party-goers were transported to central London in a limo for their big night out. As soon as the singers arrived and stepped on to the red carpet, they were greeted by flashing camera bulbs and people screaming their names. 'I could hear one person screaming my name really loudly, which made me feel really good,' Will remembers.

At the glamorous, celeb-packed after-show bash in London's hip restaurant Mezzo, he rubbed shoulders with the likes of Orlando Bloom and Josh Hartnett and nibbled on expensive canapés. It was here that Will experienced the fickle world of fame first-hand, as people he'd never met before fell over themselves to say hello and make small talk with the rising star. He decided there and then that the party circuit was not for him. Although he had a great time, he couldn't understand how people would want to do that kind of thing night after night and confessed, 'If I had a night off I'd probably choose to go for a meal with friends because it'd be more fun. I really enjoyed the premiere and I loved walking on the red carpet into the cinema. But, given the choice of the party afterwards or the chance to be down the pub with my friends, I'd go down the pub. I love my evenings because they are my time, and when I do want to pop down the pub I will.'

But *Pop Idol* wasn't simply parties and premieres. There

was the small matter of the national singing competition to consider. And the partying was soon over, come the big-band night, when a row kicked off between Simon and Pete when Simon labelled Darius's performance of 'Let's Face The Music And Dance' as his weakest yet. 'If we're not allowed to put an opinion over, what's the point of us being here?' an angry Simon told Pete, who then accused Simon of being ageist.

But sadly it wasn't just Simon who didn't rate Darius's performance, and once again the tall Scot found himself in the bottom three along with Zoe and Hayley. However, he was ultimately saved from the chop as it was Hayley who was voted off, and this time there were sobs all round – even from Nicki Chapman and *Pop Idol Extra* presenter Kate Thornton, who shared a hug with Hayley after the show.

In terms of the voting, Gareth was still edging out Will – but only just. The singing-sensation-to-be was slowly clawing back the votes. By week six, just 0.4 per cent divided the two contenders.

Week after week the show was getting tougher. The weeks in the run-up to the big final were a roller coaster of emotions for Will. On the one hand he was absolutely loving getting to perform, and receiving such incredible feedback from the judges and audience alike was a huge buzz. His confidence was growing steadily, and he was morphing into a fully fledged showman before millions of viewers' eyes.

But on the other hand, the fact that he had become close to his fellow contestants over the course of the competition meant that each week he had to say goodbye to more and more friends, as people were steadily eliminated. It was all weighing heavily on his broad shoulders.

CHAPTER THREE

And The Winner Is ...

Will had the time of his life taking part in *Pop Idol*, and the truth of how much he wanted to win really only hit him once the competition was down to the final four. Worryingly for Will, there was a very real chance that he could have left the show that week – all his hopes of walking away with the big prize would have been dashed.

Week seven was set to whittle down the remaining four contestants to just three; it was a nail-biting time. For the first time in the competition, each of the contestants was asked to sing two songs during the show, in their bid to impress the viewers. The theme of the week was number one hits.

Darius performed 'It's Not Unusual' by Tom Jones and 'Whole Again' by Atomic Kitten (which got the seal of approval from band member Natasha, who went along to see the show). Gareth belted out 'Wake Me Up Before You Go Go', by Wham!, as well as that old favourite, 'Unchained Melody'. The last lady standing, Zoe, treated the audience to Whitney Houston's 'I Wanna Dance With Somebody' and Jennifer Rush's 'The Power Of Love', while Will rounded up the evening with The Bee Gees' 'Night Fever' and The Eurythmics' 'There Must Be An Angel'. Following unenthusiastic comments from the judges after his performances, Will became convinced that his luck had run out and he would soon be waving goodbye to his dreams of stardom.

The stress of the impending result really got to Will – so much so that when he was being interviewed by presenter Kate Thornton on the companion *Pop Idol* show, *Pop Idol Extra*, on ITV2, just before the outcome was revealed, he broke down and started to cry. 'I'd had enough and I had this hideous feeling I was going to go, and truthfully I wanted to go. I'd had enough of going through this week after week. It really is hard,' he said afterwards.

Then the results were announced. It was Zoe who had impressed the judges least, and that was sadly reflected in the voting figures too. When the incredible 3.7 million votes had been counted, it was the seventeen-year-old smiler who was sent home. But Will was hardly out of the woods just yet. Though he came second in the poll with 27.9 per cent of the vote, Gareth Gates was still leading the way with an impressive 28.7 per cent. If Will was to triumph in the competition – as he so fiercely wanted – he was going to have to produce some exceptional performances in the next two weeks.

But, as always, Will was unaware of the specifics of the vote – all he knew was that he was safe for another week. When this realization hit him, he let out a huge sigh of relief. Perhaps he *could* endure a few more weeks of fear after all, he reasoned.

Backstage after the show that night, there was further excitement when Will discovered that he had been watched during his performance by none other than Annie Lennox. 'The funny thing was, my family and I were backstage and we ran towards each other when we saw her and all said at the same time, "Annie Lennox is here!"' Will laughs.

Will had the support of his family behind him week after

week. In fact, at times it seemed like they were more nervous than him. Will's dad Robin recalls how amazing it felt seeing his son up on stage – and doing such an incredible job. 'I couldn't believe how good he was, I really couldn't. His performance was fabulous. I was very nervous about being in the audience but Will was very good at hiding his nerves – although I did see the microphone shaking a bit more than usual. It takes a huge amount of guts to sing in front of all those people. The pressure on those young singers was incredible.'

And there was no keeping Will's twin brother Rupert away from the live shows. 'Rupert has gone every week and he can't wait to get there. It's like a party every Saturday night,' laughed Robin.

But it was a party with a poisonous side. With the show now down to the final three, Will started to panic again. When the remaining finalists – Will, Darius and Gareth – were recording what would become the first ever *Pop Idol* single, Will had an attack of insecurity. The trio recorded the double A-sided 'Evergreen'/'Anything Is Possible' at west London's Olympic studios – which have played host to top bands like the Rolling Stones and Oasis – but Will felt uncomfortable during the recording and soon realized that he hated 'Evergreen' with a passion.

Will says honestly: 'It almost felt like the songs had been chosen especially for Gareth. I had never sung a song like that throughout the entire show, so I think it was obvious it wasn't for me. [Both songs] were great pop music, but written in a style more to suit his voice. I'd be lying if I said I didn't think the winner had already been decided.'

He also declared later that Gareth was going to win the contest, no question. Will was convinced that the audience reactions to Gareth's performances meant a triumph for the teenager was already a done deal.

On top of Will's personal insecurities, the newspaper headlines were also getting to him. Although he had promised himself that he wouldn't read what the tabloids had to say, he couldn't help having the odd look every now and again. He discovered that the *Sun* newspaper was heavily backing Gareth to win – and that his younger competitor had been the bookies' favourite for several weeks running.

'It was a really difficult time for me. Things got to me,' Will reflects. 'There had been all these polls and stories in the papers claiming Gareth was the outright winner. Things just got a bit too much for me. I think I got sucked into the hype that he would win and it was decided. I even had friends call me and say, "Gareth is going to win." So when we were asked along to the recording studio to record "Evergreen" and I heard it was a Westlife song, it really hit me. I just thought, "This is a song he would sing – not me." I struggled with the song and they knew this. But I worked hard and made the song my own.'

Will may have found his first experience in a proper recording studio daunting, but unbeknown to him Simon Cowell was confident that the rising star had managed to put his own stamp on the tracks and had done a great job. 'Will was a little bit nervous, but within about five minutes this huge Will grin appeared, as if to say, "He's right, I can make it my own,"' remembers Simon.

Once the recording was complete, Simon was so impressed by everyone's performances on the day that the music guru made the extremely confident claim: 'If I haven't got a number one record I'm going to eat my very, very high-waisted trousers.'

As well as the excitement of working in a recording studio, Darius, Will and Gareth got their first taste of major stardom the very same week, when they were invited to support S Club 7 in Dublin on the first night of their UK tour.

All three lads performed the tracks they had sung on the previous Saturday's show, and Ant and Dec flew over specially to introduce them. 'Darius went first and I was standing backstage watching him, absolutely terrified!' recalls Will. 'As Darius came off, Dec went on and introduced me to the audience ...' Mr Young then performed live to thousands of people for the very first time. An elated Will said afterwards, 'Words really cannot explain that feeling when you walk on stage!'

However, as had been the case all the way through the competition, the highs of the week soon paled against the pressure of the Saturday night sing-off. And this was by far the tensest week of the contest. The initial 10,000 aspiring Pop Idols had been reduced to the final three, but it was now time for either Gareth, Darius or Will to say their goodbyes, in the second-to-last live show.

It was undoubtedly Will's most stressful week to date, largely because when he stepped out on to the stage to sing Bobby Darin's 'Beyond The Sea', his nerves took over and he momentarily forgot the words. With everything but the right words swimming around his head, Will hurriedly contemplated what messing up now would do to his chances of winning the competition. 'I'd never admitted to myself before how much I wanted to get to that final. It scared me how much I wanted it all,' he reveals.

Suddenly, from nowhere, the words popped back into Will's brain and he pulled off yet another of his stellar performances, impressing the judges no end. An excited Dr Fox told him afterwards: 'Do you know, Will, you're brilliant. You know I love your voice. Your effortless style is good. But do you know, the people in the music business have been giving us a hard time about this programme, saying it's not the way we should be finding talent. And I would like to say here in front of thirteen, fourteen million people that we have three great singers and six amazing songs tonight. This is what it's all about. It's fantastic. Well done.'

All three lads gave great performances, but the nature of the competition meant that someone had to go. Tonight it was Darius's turn, and he took his defeat well. With 20.9 per cent of the vote, Darius fought a good fight. But it was the other figures that mattered more: Will, by a whisker, pipped Gareth with just 0.5 per cent of the vote. But as had happened before, the balance could easily shift. There were now only two contestants left. But there could only be one winner.

In the days leading up to the grand final, Will discovered the true power of the press and what a huge effect it can have on the public. Gossip was rife all week, especially after claims that tensions were simmering behind the scenes between the two front-runners. There were reports that Gareth's parents had moaned that Will's parents didn't get involved during the show, or sing and dance along like everyone else. Immediately, an upset Will hit back: 'It's not true. My mum says you can see them dancing on the telly!'

Gareth also went on the record to deny that his parents had ever made the claims, and the dispute was soon settled. While the press were no doubt hoping to create some tension between the last men standing, Will says that, if anything, the whole episode brought the families together and made them closer than ever.

Will also maintained that, even though he and Gareth were both desperate to win the coveted *Pop Idol* prize – a record contract with BMG, a guaranteed deal with management company 19, and the chance to headline the *Pop Idol* UK tour – there was no real rivalry between them.

'Gareth and I have really bonded over the last two weeks. We're not competitive,' he said.

In fact, Will revealed that he had great admiration for Gareth, who had battled with a crippling stutter throughout the show. 'I really respect Gareth. I never thought about his stutter being so difficult for him, and never thought we were similar as people. But now I think we could remain friends after the show.'

As the competition neared its end, Will admitted that he finally felt like a real, bona fide vocalist. 'I feel like a singer and I can say to people that I'm a singer,' he said proudly. 'I'd never have said that before, because I'd think people's eyes would glaze over and they'd just say, "Right."'

Now all he had to do was prove to the public that he was the singer they should choose as their Pop Idol. It was an aim requiring some intense hard work and non-stop dedication. The week before the final show, Gareth and Will toured the country on specially designed *Pop Idol* buses emblazoned with their images. They held a competition throughout to see who could blag the best freebies, and Will was close to being victorious when he walked off with a life-size model of Lara Croft. He'd spotted it at Radio 1 following an interview with Chris Moyles, who was openly a huge fan of his. However, Will's joy was cut short when radio bosses demanded that he hand back the cardboard cut-out, and he begrudgingly returned it with a sigh.

The tour was run like a political campaign, and both lads made countless media appearances throughout the week, in order to promote themselves to the nation. The duo completed around one hundred interviews for radio, TV and press as part of their individual campaigns, as well as meeting thousands of adoring fans. They also had the Prime Minister's security guards on hand, in case anyone became a touch overexcited at the sight of the two most talked-about people in Britain.

During one interview Will said, 'It's incredible being part of this. I'm loving every single minute. I was convinced I was going to get kicked off the show on Saturday. It was nerve-racking. You get fatalistic and have to protect yourself by getting into a certain frame of mind. But I know I'm going to have a go and do my best. Let battle commence. I am who I am and that's my appeal. I would say if you enjoy my performances, then vote for me.'

Even though the object of the manic press attack was to win votes and influence people, Will and Gareth took it all in their stride and didn't let it affect their friendship. They spent much of their time texting each other to see how they were getting on, and also met for drinks to catch up at several points during the week. They may have been in fierce competition, but that didn't mean that they couldn't still get along.

When at last the campaign trail came to an end, Will managed to snatch a bit of time off – and he had planned exactly how he wanted to spend it. 'I did a radio interview at 8 a.m. and then I went back to bed, which was a real luxury. I saw some friends this afternoon. It's the first time that I have had the chance to see them properly for quite a while,' he revealed. 'I'm not exhausted, though. I'm surviving on lots of adrenaline at the moment. This is the most thrilling thing I have done in my life.'

After a very long, tiring week, it was finally time to take to the stage. The final of one of the biggest and most exciting singing competitions the UK had ever seen was about to begin.

With the likes of Noel Gallagher, Robbie Williams and Posh and Becks apparently gunning for Will (Victoria said of the final: 'To get as far in the competition as they have, they must both be very talented. But I must admit I have a soft spot for Will and he looks such a nice guy'), Will had some serious backing behind him. Kylie Minogue also sent a 'good luck' message to a thrilled Mr Young. 'That was the best thing,' Will said, smiling. 'I've been a fan for ages. Her first album, where she sang "I Should Be So Lucky", was one of the first albums I ever bought.'

In addition to the celebrity support, of course, were his lucky pants, which were to be his secret weapon on stage. 'I have been wearing my lucky black boxer shorts since the start of *Pop Idol*,' Will confirmed. 'Don't get me wrong, though. I'm not some dirty guy. I have been washing them myself every day since the contest started four months ago.'

On the subject of why people should vote for him, Will said humbly: 'I hope that the audience can see I'm still Will and I haven't changed. I just hope that my voice will make people want to pick up the phone and vote.'

Gracing the Green Room on the night were celebrities including Ricky Gervais, Tamzin Outhwaite, Charlotte Church, Brian Dowling, Annie Lennox, Gary Lucy and Sean Hughes. Back out front, Will and Gareth flags were being waved frantically by the audience and the finalists' nervous friends and family, who were there to show their support. The entire studio was on tenterhooks, as the moment of truth edged ever closer. But first came the performances that would determine the fates of the final two.

Graham Norton had tossed a coin earlier in the week to see who would perform first. Will won, meaning that he would be first to face the judging panel and the all-important public. As soon as the show began, at 7.10 p.m., he blew everyone away with his rendition of The Doors' 'Light My Fire', and he went on to showcase the first ever *Pop Idol* single, the double A-sided 'Evergreen'/'Anything Is Possible'.

'You are a multi-faceted performer tonight, you really are,' Nicki told him. '[You've come] from vague auditions in the early stages to what I see in front of me tonight: a true superstar.'

Simon added: 'Will, we're going to be working together so I'm going to be nice to you. I was wrong earlier on, I am happy to admit it. We're not always right in this business, but you totally deserve your place here tonight. You are a superstar as Nicki said – congratulations!'

Despite this rapturous response, Will wasn't home and dry yet. His rival, the ever-popular Gareth Gates, also rose to the challenge admirably – and then there was nothing for the singers to do but wait. After Gareth's well-received performances of the double A-sided single and Westlife's 'Flying Without Wings', the show took a break while the votes were collated and counted. During this time Will did his best to stay calm and focused. An interview with Kate Thornton helped to take his mind off things slightly, but when he and Gareth were told that the voting was incredibly close, and that the lead had been swapping constantly throughout the evening, their anxiety levels rose again.

There was also tension when the judges chose final night to air one of their many disagreements. This time the hostility was between Pete Waterman and Simon Cowell. Astonishingly, Pete claimed that Will had only made it into the final fifty because there weren't enough boys in the competition. Simon angrily fought Will's corner, and the pair exchanged some harsh words backstage – which didn't make for the best atmosphere when it was time for the winner to be announced.

At 10.20 p.m., the results were in. Will and Gareth nervously took their places on stage as the competition reached its climax. Over six months of hard work, perseverance and pressure all boiled down to this one moment. The two finalists gave each other a supportive hug and then both stood anxiously side by side on the stage, waiting to hear the result. They were resplendent in their chic suits – Gareth in dazzling white and Will in a rather more sober navy – and both looked like true stars.

Viewers had been so desperate to vote in the final that the National Grid had called ITV earlier in the evening to check what time the advert breaks would take place. They had to ensure that they were equipped to deal with what they knew would be a huge surge in electricity, which could potentially cause power cuts. And they were right to worry. The show's hosts, Ant and Dec, announced that the competition had registered a breathtaking 8.7 million votes over the course of the evening. It was a new British record, which now has pride of place in the *Guinness Book of Records*.

The statistical formalities over, it was time to get down to business. After what seemed like an eternity, it was revealed that the very deserving winner – by a whisker – was an incredibly stunned William Young, with 4.6 million votes and 53.1 per cent of the overall vote.

Instantly, the studio was buzzing with screams, cheers and many tears, as Will clasped his hands to his face and started to cry. Will had practically resigned himself to the fact that he would come second, which made host Ant's revelation that he was the victor all the more shocking to him. 'When he said what the votes were, I thought, "I am second and I have lost by that much." I just thought, "Oh well, that's not bad." I promise that's what I thought. I felt isolated – then when I heard I'd won it was like I suddenly woke up. I felt like I'd been hit. I could not believe it.

'When I went into the competition, I remember thinking, "Who's ever going to vote for a middle-class, gay, slightly eccentric Frank Spencer lookalike student, who sings jazz and soul?"'

As it turned out, 4.6 million people.

Will and a very gracious Gareth hugged immediately after Will's win, with the runner-up saying generously, 'Well done, mate, you're fantastic!' Gareth continued, 'Will is just absolutely wonderful. I must say that he is an absolutely awesome guy. If there's one person who really deserves it, it's Will. We are really good friends.'

Will then took to the stage to sing 'Evergreen', while the rest of the final fifty contestants swarmed around him. When the song was over, Darius and several other burly men lifted Will up on to their shoulders and, with a smile the size of the Grand Canyon, the winner waved at the overjoyed audience.

'I am absolutely ecstatic,' Will said afterwards. 'I've always wanted to do this and throughout the competition it felt more and more right. I am so ready for it. I am just up for it massively.'

After the strain of the evening, it was time for Will to head off into the night to celebrate what had been an incredible evening, safe in the knowledge that he was Britain's new Pop Idol.

The show's producers threw a huge bash backstage, where Will was joined by Gareth, loads of other *Pop Idol* contestants, a fair smattering of celebs, and of course his beloved family. Will's twin brother Rupert was one of the first to congratulate him, and he couldn't have been happier. 'We were all geared up for Mr Gates to win, because that's what the press were saying,' Rupert admitted. 'Then we were whisked off into a room, and we were all crying. We all had to do interviews – plus drink loads of champagne! All of the families got on really well together. We were always exchanging gifts and supporting each other. Will knew he had a talent – and had the confidence to win it!'

After the backstage party, Will, his family and his friends all headed to a nearby hotel to continue the festivities. His parents had hired a swish suite specially – Will's dad paying for the do with the £800 he had won at the bookies, from the bet he'd placed on Will winning the show!

As Will partied the night away, he was conscious that he was expected to be up early to start his official Pop Idol duties the next morning. He was going to have to do them with a raging hangover. But, boy, was it going to be worth it.

CHAPTER FOUR

Friends And Family

Will comes from a close-knit family, and they were his biggest supporters throughout *Pop Idol*. They could clearly be seen in the crowd clapping and cheering Will on every week.

He is best friends with his twin brother Rupert and older sister Emma (who has a young son called Jack), totally adores his parents Robin and Annabel, and describes grandmother Meme as 'one of the loves of my life'. He joked during *Pop Idol*, 'I signed my first autograph the other day. It was for my grandma, but that doesn't matter!'

Will was also very close to his grandfather on his mum's side, Robert Griffith, who died shortly before *Pop Idol* began. He still misses him terribly today. 'My grandfather was so important to me. He taught me many things – he was such a gentleman. I think he helped shape my personality. He taught me to always be polite and well mannered. He was real old school. Shoes were very important to him. He'd say, "Always make sure they're shiny and clean." In fact, when I did the big-band song in the show, I was wearing his cufflinks and his watch and I made sure my shoes were spotless! He loved his family and was incredibly supportive. I don't know what he'd make of my life now if he were alive. One of the nicest things I was able to do was write a letter to him before he died, telling him what he meant to me. A lot of people never get that chance.'

Will dedicated a book charting his success, *Anything is Possible*, to Robert, writing: 'To Bobby, my grandfather and a man who I loved and respected from day one, even when he made me eat brussel sprouts and broccoli! He will never leave my memory or my heart. I will love him to the day I die.'

Sadly, Will never got to meet his other grandfather, his dad's dad Digby Aretas Young, who was a long-serving member of the RAF, as he died in 1966 at the age of fifty.

Will's ancestors on his father's side were an interesting bunch by all accounts. Although Will doesn't talk about them very often, there is a great story behind them. Back in the eighteenth and nineteenth centuries, most of Will's relatives were members of the armed forces – a career that has always been a great tradition in the family, harking right back to Will's great-great-great-great-grandfather, Sir Aretas William Young, who joined up back in 1795, when he was just seventeen. He served in Ireland, Egypt and even fought the French in the Peninsular War. He was later posted to Trinidad, where he eventually took charge of Trinidad's government. In 1826, Aretas moved to Demerara – which these days is known as Guyana – where he was appointed protector of slaves. Five years later he became the governor of Prince Edward Island in Canada, and in 1834 all his hard work was rewarded when he was knighted by King William IV. He and his wife, Sarah Cox, had seven children together, four of whom joined the army. At the age of fifty-seven, in 1835, Aretas passed away.

The legacy then continued in his son Henry, who took a job in the colonial treasury when he was nineteen. In the 1830s he was stationed in Demerara and continued the work that his father had started, helping to release slaves.

In 1848, Henry became governor of South Australia and later Tasmania, and in 1847 he once again followed in his father's footsteps when he was knighted. Eventually, he retired and moved back to London, where he lived a happy life until he died in 1870, aged sixty-eight. People may make jokes about how well-to-do Will is, but when you look at his impressive background, you can certainly see where he gets his determination and level-headedness from.

Will totally adores his family and they, in turn, think the world of the ever-smiling lad who has become the nation's idol – but they don't treat him any differently from the way they did before his win. 'I'm just the middle son in the family. I still get told to tidy my room!' Will laughs. Though it's true that he initially kept his involvement in *Pop Idol* a closely guarded secret from his family, in case it didn't come to anything, he always knew that they would totally understand his desire to try his luck. And once he got down to the final fifty and came clean to them, they instantly became his biggest and most loyal supporters.

No one is prouder of Will than his dad, despite the fact that Robin had originally advised his son against a career in the entertainment industry. 'I was humbled when I first saw him on the show. I'd underestimated his ability and strength of character. I'm so glad he ignored my advice,' says Robin today.

Will credits his family for keeping him down-to-earth throughout the competition and beyond, saying, 'My family wouldn't let me get big-headed. We're just not like that. It's always hard when you enter into a new way of life or career because the chances are that you will change slightly. I think that my family were worried at first, but as time has gone on they have realized I'm still the same Will. I've actually been very, very lucky because my family have been fantastic. They've always supported me in my choices and have only

Looking suave and debonair for a photo shoot during *Pop Idol*, Will Young is every inch the old boy from his former school, the prestigious Wellington College (*inset*).

Would you put your fate in their hands? From left to right, *Pop Idol* judges Simon Cowell, Pete Waterman, Nicki Chapman and 'Dr Fox'.

From 10,000 applicants to the final ten: the lucky singers who made it through the judges' and the viewers' votes to continue their bid for stardom in the show's live heats. Back row, l-r: Gareth Gates, Zoe Birkett, Darius Danesh, Jessica Garlick, Will Young. Front row, l-r: Korben, Hayley Evetts, Laura Doherty, Rosie Ribbons, Aaron Bayley.

Will at his first ever film premiere, glammed up to the max. From l-r, Gareth, Hayley, Darius, Zoe and Will all attend the celebrity screening of *Black Hawk Down*, partying afterwards at London's trendy Mezzo restaurant.

There can only be one winner: the *Pop Idol* finalists battle it out on the campaign trail, in the very last week of the show.

Will Young *is* the nation's Pop Idol.

Pop Idol hosts Ant and Dec celebrate with the newly-crowned Idol. The revelry continued until 6 a.m. the following morning.

OPPOSITE PAGE: Taking it all in: Will in Cuba filming the videos for his debut single.

Life will never be the same again: Will's fans queue to meet their idol.

Will shares a joke with fellow *Pop Idol* finalists Darius and Gareth at *Record of the Year 2002*. Will's debut single, 'Evergreen'/'Anything is Possible' was nominated for the award; the single sold a record-breaking 1.1 million copies in its first week on sale alone.

Will meets and greets his public (*above*);
launching his debut album, *From Now On*,
on 7 October 2002 (*right*).

OVER PAGE: Will doing what he does best.

ever wanted what's best for me. We're very close but at the same time we all respect the fact that we need our own space too. We all live for the moment.'

Will acts the same as he's always done around his family, and they know that he'll never morph into a stereotype of a pampered pop star – especially as he still manages to do the odd embarrassing thing in front of his family when drunk. 'I rang up my mum to say I was very upset that she was going to get old, and that I wouldn't put her in a home. It was about 1 a.m. though!' Will reveals.

With fame comes problems, and Will's family were understandably worried about what effect his sudden stardom would have on them. Before Will's *Pop Idol* win, Robin commented, 'I'll support him in his decision as long as it doesn't interfere with our lives too much. It really hit us how much things had changed when we were called up by a firm recently offering us advice on security, should Will become famous. I can't have a conversation with anyone about anything apart from *Pop Idol*. My clients ring up and congratulate me about William. All they want to talk about is the show.'

When the fame did start to kick off in a big way, it was Will's family who were at the forefront of his mind. 'At the end of the day, it's my family I'm worried about,' he said. 'For me it's a chance to take on another of life's challenges. This is what I've always wanted to do and now I'm doing it. I know there are going to be bad times, but I've got the guts and courage to deal with them when they arrive – I hope! I'm sure my family will rise to the occasion too – I've seen them do that before.'

And he wasn't wrong. Robin and Annabel were determined that they would carry on with their day-to-day lives, and mum Annabel was especially keen to maintain her privacy in the face of her son's fame. She said, 'It's William's thing. We're really not keen to be involved.'

But while Rupert is also keen to stay out of the spotlight, he enjoyed taking the *Pop Idol* ride with Will. However, he was both glad and relieved when it came to an end. 'It's been a roller coaster, really. Being in the studio and getting involved with the whole thing has been a very unique experience. Surreal, really. It's amazing because it brought the family closer towards the end, though we all really wanted it to be over.'

Will says that twin brother Rupert has been a constant support throughout his life. He reveals that the pair are like chalk and cheese, with totally different dreams and aspirations, and there is no jealousy whatsoever on Rupert's part when it comes to Will's success. 'We've always been individuals in our own right and will both go our separate ways in life,' Will explains. 'Apart from being my brother, Rupert is one of my best friends. We're very close and I know him better than anyone else in the whole world.'

As for Rupert, he says that he's always had faith in Will's performing abilities. 'I always thought he'd end up on stage. We can't wait for his album to come out. I've heard bits of it and it's very good. Different, funky, jazzy, cool.'

Regardless of Rupert's enthusiasm, though, don't expect the pair to team up for a duet any time soon. 'Believe me, you will never see us duetting,' laughs Will. 'Even when times are tough and I need a gimmick! No danger of us being the new Bros!'

Will's second family is his large network of friends, to whom he is incredibly close and who have been, happily, totally unfazed by his fame. 'All my friends and family have just been fantastic, really,' Will commented shortly after winning *Pop Idol*. 'Another thing that's kept my feet on the ground is that I did go to university and did go through life experiences there, and made really good friends, and they're just not fazed by it and their excitement washes off on me as well.

'They are incredibly supportive and, thankfully, I've not had vague acquaintances crawling out of the woodwork trying to get in touch with me since I won *Pop Idol*. They know that I'd see through them right away.'

Will still keeps in touch with his friends from university as often as he can, and is keen to carry on doing the same things they did together when they were students. 'I spent the whole weekend with them,' he said, a few weeks after his talent-show triumph. 'I went to the rugby, I went to Twickenham and watched the rugby with a friend and my brother.

'Things have changed in terms of becoming a public face but I still go out for pizza with my mates, I promise you. I still go out for a drink, still go to the park, but people recognize me and no one ever recognized me before. I'm still the same person, I still have the same family, friends, still live in the same place. I've just gained a lot of things. The best thing about it is actually working for a living. I spent so long in education and was thinking, "How am I going to get a job and how am I going to sing?" Now I'm singing as a job – it's perfect for me, it's a dream come true! My friends sometimes catch me grinning and they say, "You're really enjoying this *Pop Idol* thing, aren't you?" and I just laugh, because I really am. This is my dream.'

There's no doubting that when someone becomes famous, very often the people around them change overnight. They either want to ride on the celebrity's coat-tails and become very showbizzy, or they find that they can't handle all the new attention and the friendship fizzles out. However, Will reports that the majority of his friends haven't found his stardom difficult to deal with, and in fact their friendships have become even stronger because of the extraordinary scenario. Will knows that he can turn to them at any time for help and advice, and that they're not hanging around with him for the glory. 'I think my relationships with my friends have become closer since doing the show. Definitely. When I was doing *Pop Idol* that was all the conversation would be about. But now, as things get less new and we all get used to it, we just talk about our jobs, and I've become more conscious not to talk about it. I think I see more of my friends now than I used to before. You just need your friends big time.'

But surely they must treat him differently sometimes? 'My friends are still as abusive to me as ever!' he laughs. 'I'm not really the kind of person, though, who would like to be treated like a star and have an army of minders or anything like that. If that ever started happening, I'd probably just turn around and politely say, "Please, don't." '

In many respects, though, Will's remarkable achievement on *Pop Idol* wasn't entirely unexpected. His mates had more than an inkling that he might one day be a star. As he explains: 'All my friends knew all I wanted to do was sing, so it's not strange for them to see me doing what I've always wanted to do.'

Yet as much as he totally trusts his mates, Will did have to have a serious chat with them about the media side of things. Sometimes private things can make their way inadvertently into the papers via a friend. There is always someone willing to offer money for stars' secrets, and it's easy to slip up and say things to strangers in a friendly fashion, without realizing that they are members of the press. 'There's a whole secrecy thing, which was an odd conversation to have with them at first,' Will admits. 'You need to have that conversation because this is a funny business that I'm in.

'But I think you can remain a private person if you want to. Fame is a value you put on yourself. You don't necessarily need five bouncers and three cars to go to the chemist.'

Thankfully Will knows that his friends would never betray him and that they're there for him if he needs them. Because the TV show was so stressful, Will leant on his friends for support during that pressured time – and they never once let him down. He's keen to reciprocate that support, and always strives to give the best possible advice to his mates.

He is also careful when it comes to making new friends, and knows the kind of people he won't necessarily get on with. 'People who are obsessed with material stuff. Or people trying so desperately to be "cool", who think it is important to drive the right car and go to the right bars. I do like that, actually, but I can see the relativity of it. Family, friends and people in my neighbourhood who treat me well are much more important for me. My friends do have that in common. They are very different from each other, but they are all nice people. I don't want to see rude behaviour around me.'

Despite the media constantly trying to stir up trouble between Gareth Gates and Will during *Pop Idol*, the pair remain good friends to this day. Even in the nerve-racking final, judge Nicki paid homage to their dedication to one another. 'You have both been sensational tonight, you really have,' Nicki told them. 'And you know how strong your friendship is. This week you've been loyal to each other and that is unique. Keep grounded. You deserve the success.'

It's clear to see that Will will do his best to stay down-to-earth, no matter how famous and successful he becomes. And it's also apparent that he will stay in touch with his beloved family and fantastic friends as much as possible, however busy and hectic his lifestyle.

'Without doubt, I think the most difficult part of being famous is the way it has touched everyone close in my life. My family and friends don't treat me any differently. There are a few who are quite insecure about me staying in touch. You know, those friends who are like, "You never ring me." But I really do have a valid excuse for not calling them as often as I should. It's not intentional. I'm still the same Will I've always been. Just a few more people know me now, and I'm a little busier!

'I'll never lose sight of the fact that I'm surrounded by a brilliant family and group of friends. Being a millionaire will never change the way I am to these people,' says Mr Young.

With his huge success now an ever-present aspect of Will's life, such stability and support is truly priceless.

CHAPTER FIVE

First Week, Fresh Start

On the Sunday morning after his big win, Will woke up feeling less than peachy, which was hardly surprising considering he'd had only two hours' sleep thanks to the previous night's celebrations.

With a thick head and a mere five minutes to pack his bag before he had to head to Heathrow, Will was getting his first real taste of the pop-star life. He would soon be leaving behind the mania of *Pop Idol* and jetting off to sunnier climes for his first ever video shoot, and the work was set to start immediately. 'We didn't stop until about 1 a.m. on Saturday night, and then I had my family and friends back to the hotel and we stayed up chatting until about 6 a.m.,' admitted a tired Will, who wasn't allowed a moment's shut-eye even in the taxi on the way to the airport: the journey was instead spent giving magazine interviews, as it was the only time Will had to squeeze them into his already packed schedule.

On his arrival at Heathrow airport, Will was instantly recognized by some eagle-eyed fans, and ended up signing autographs for travellers and staff alike. Then it was time for a fried breakfast to set himself up for the flight. With last night's booze still charging around his body, he needed to eat something to settle his stomach and perk him up before the long journey.

This was to be Will's first week as the nation's newly crowned Pop Idol. And what better place to spend it than in exotic Cuba? 'It was a twelve-hour flight, but we were in business class. It was very exciting. I think I was being very annoying with my moving chair – I just kept pressing the button to move the back of the seat upright and all the way back again. But, hey, I'd never flown club class before,' said a sleepy but elated Will.

After grabbing forty winks on the plane, Will and his new personal assistant Faye touched down in Cuba and checked into the swanky five-star Nacional Hotel in Havana. As the place to start his new life as an international pop star, the exclusive establishment really didn't disappoint.

The next morning was spent having a late breakfast, and then Will – delighted at having a few days off before the video shoot started – took the opportunity to reflect on the crazy last few months of his life. *Pop Idol* had lasted for nearly half a year, and Will needed time to take in the fact that he had won the show. 'It has, without doubt, been the most strange, challenging, character-testing, exciting, extreme journey I've been on in my life,' he mused.

But he wasn't finding his new life that easy to adjust to. 'When I was whisked off to Cuba straight after *Pop Idol* to film my video, I did get lonely,' he confided later. 'I had never thought about winning the show and then, hours later, I'm on a plane to Cuba. I had someone from the management company with me, but things were a bit awkward to begin with. There were people there, but I just didn't know them. I ended up getting on with these people really well, thankfully. I think I can look ahead and foresee moments when things might get lonely and then I'll know who to lean on.'

Will was keen to take in some of the local culture, and took the opportunity to visit some tourist attractions and national parks during the day. But back home, the rest of the Young clan weren't having quite such a restful time of it. The press were desperate to talk to Will's family to get their views on his win, and the news filtered through to Will that there were journalists and cameramen camped outside his parents' Hungerford home. 'That really upset me and made me feel incredibly guilty, because *I* entered this competition, *not* my family, and now I'm thousands of miles away and I've left them at home to deal with all the frenzy,' said a concerned Will.

The worry of this, on top of a heavy dose of jet-leg and the loneliness he was feeling, made Will's first day in Cuba a rather strange and contemplative one. But Tuesday was an altogether better day, as Will had a long lie-in before heading out to the countryside to take in some of the stunning views that Havana had to offer. The extra sleep filled him with energy and enthusiasm, and he revealed eagerly, 'Today I climbed a mountain and drank fresh coconut juice!'

In addition to this adventure, Will's friend Milsy (Camilla) arrived on the Tuesday to join him in Cuba, which instantly made the new star feel more relaxed and at home in his strange surroundings. In fact, he was so pleased to see her that the pair talked for hours and hours about the weirdness of the situation, as Will tried once again to come to terms with his bizarre new life.

But it wasn't all serious talk. The friends also managed to fit in a bit of partying. 'Me and the gang decided to celebrate by drinking cocktails called Mojitos – they're pronounced Mo-hitos. I'd never had one before but I found out how you make them, so now I'm the master Mojito man! I can't remember how many we drank, but we went out at around 7 p.m. and we didn't get back until around gone three,' he revealed to the

Sun newspaper. 'That's quite a session. To be honest, I think we all overdid it because the next morning I couldn't open my eyes and my head felt as if somebody had dropped a huge weight on it.'

The night before, however, it had been a different story. Will really let his hair down and simply enjoyed the fantastic Cuban nightlife. 'I danced for England at the club – on the tables, anywhere I could. Cubans can really dance so we were trying to keep up with them and knocking back the drinks, but I think the heat eventually got the better of me and I had to sit down,' says Will.

And even in the middle of Cuba, Will was recognized. He recalls, 'This British couple came up to me and asked me who won *Pop Idol*. They'd been out for a few weeks and missed the final. I just couldn't stop smiling and I pointed at myself. It was really weird. There I was, thousands of miles away, and somebody asked me about the show. I still can't believe how huge the show became.'

Wednesday was Will's last day of relaxing before the real work began, and he took full advantage of it by doing a spot of chilled-out shopping, picking up presents for his friends and family. He and Milsy also went for lunch in one of Havana's incredible squares and were treated to some authentic local music. They rounded off the day by going to see a popular Havana-based band called Buena Vista Social Club, who were playing in a nearby club. Despite the great entertainment, Will made sure he got to bed at a sensible time. 'We went to bed at a reasonable hour, because work starts tomorrow,' he admitted. He was learning fast.

Back in England, Simon Cowell had given an interview which acknowledged that he had wanted Gareth to win *Pop Idol*, much to many people's dismay. But despite his declaration, he did still manage to heap some very deserving praise on Will. 'Yes, I wanted Gareth to win,' Simon said. 'I wanted to keep my integrity as a judge and I couldn't suddenly switch to [supporting] Will when I felt he was going to win. But was I glad Gareth lost? No. He was numb afterwards, but then it sank in that it was the beginning of the rest of his life. Will gave the performance of his life on the single "Evergreen". It was one of the best bits of TV I've ever seen.'

Simon also suggested that Will was about to discover what the singer was already beginning to suspect – that pop stardom was going to be no walk in the park. 'The work starts here,' Simon commented with a smile.

On Thursday 14 February, St Valentine's Day, it was time for Will to find out exactly what making a video entailed. He was filming two videos in Cuba; one for 'Evergreen' and another for 'Anything Is Possible'.

After a painful 5 a.m. start, it was straight into styling and make-up, and then work began on the 'Anything Is Possible' shoot. It was filmed in two locations – some old ruins and a deserted park. And while both sites were beautiful, the crew soon discovered that they'd brought the British weather with them when it started to pour down. Still, Will managed to stay optimistic and decided that the shower would add to the atmosphere. He wasn't about to let a little thing like rain get him down. Or the fact that it was a twelve-hour shoot, and there wasn't a lot of time for tea breaks. 'It was hard work but great fun,' Will said of his first video-shoot experience.

Although he was feeling shattered from the previous day's long schedule, Will was up at 9 a.m. on the Friday to start filming the video for 'Evergreen', which was set inside a beautiful old Havana theatre. Even though things were a bit rushed, Will loved every minute of his second video experience and said: 'Most artists come out for a week to somewhere like this and shoot one video, but I've had to do two in the same time so it's been manic. We were doing twelve-hour days and in this heat that can be a killer, but I wouldn't want to be doing anything else.'

For although Will's schedule in Cuba was busy, it was still a welcome break from the relentlessness of the *Pop Idol* heats. 'Things did get frantic – especially in the last couple of weeks of the show,' Will revealed. 'For me, the show was always about my singing. I got through to the final ten and I got to sing my favourite songs. It was always about this. But as the show went on, it became clear that, with all the media attention, everyone was talking about us and wanted to know more about us. At the time, it was quite [pressured]. I think the best thing about the show was that the viewers saw us as who we were. From start to finish, the whole *Pop Idol* phenomenon was something I don't think anyone had ever seen before. It was unique. It was mad, but in a nice way. But it's settling down now. I really don't see me walking around with a load of minders like Madonna. It's not me. I will carry on being me for as long as I can.'

Come Saturday, it was once again time for another shoot, so the crew headed to the beach to film some footage for 'Anything Is Possible'. Will was flying home the next day, and despite his first week as a Pop Idol being nearly done and dusted, he was still having a hard time getting used to being treated differently by the people around him. 'I've been trying to buy a toothbrush and people around me keep saying, "Don't worry, we'll get it for you!"' laughed Will. 'I still can't get my head around being a pop star. Things still haven't sunk in about winning *Pop Idol*. I keep thinking I'm dreaming and I'm going to wake up to find it was all in my head.'

But he was certainly ready to face whatever challenges lay ahead. 'Before all this, I feel life had grounded me. I'd had character tests. I'd made wonderful friends at university. I'd already found out who I was,' said Will. 'I suspect for people who don't know who they are, this is probably the worst industry to go into, but I've gone into it pretty much being me all along. I think that came across in the show when I spoke up for myself.'

As Sunday dawned so did the date of Will's departure from beautiful Cuba. After the excitement and steep learning curve of his first ever video shoot, it was time for Will to head home, but when he reached the airport he discovered that his flight had been cancelled. He was expected back in the UK to film the *Pop Idol Winner's Show* with the rest of the final ten, so it was imperative that he got on another flight as soon as possible.

Thankfully, one was found for him and he was soon on his way, but his journey went far from smoothly. Terrible turbulence meant that the air hostesses couldn't serve anyone food, so Will decided that his only option was to sleep. He curled up on his seat and snoozed all the way to his stopover in France. He was already becoming skilled at grabbing some shut-eye wherever he could.

When he eventually got back to the UK, Will was in a reflective mood once again. 'Sometimes I think, "Oh no, what have I done? My life will never be the same,"' he mused, 'but I suppose it's better simply to go with the instinct that took you to that place – the thing that said inside of you: "This is right for me." Whatever bad times and good times are coming my way, I am ready for them.'

While Will was away in Cuba filming the videos for 'Evergreen' and 'Anything Is Possible', back home in England the country was still buzzing about *Pop Idol*. But Will wasn't letting the attention go to his head. The first thing he did on hitting British soil again was to drive straight to his west London flat and order in pizza with his good friend Mary. Sometimes all you need are your home comforts and good company, while the world around you is going crazy.

Meanwhile, Pete Waterman had been talking to the press a lot during Will's absence. The record producer had obviously been feeling shady about his comments during the *Pop Idol* final that Will had made it through to the final fifty only because of a lack of decent male contestants, and had subsequently been singing Will's praises at every opportunity. 'Will's single could outsell Hear'Say's debut single "Pure And Simple",' Pete gushed. 'The response to the show has been beyond anyone's expectations, so Will may become a bigger star than was ever thought possible. The world's his oyster. If he plays his cards right, he'll be here for a long time. He's very talented and has a great voice. He's already a household name and the rest, as they say, will be history.'

At the same time, the press were keen to know everything about Will and were throwing questions at him left, right and centre …

Are you planning to make any changes to your image now you're a bona fide pop idol?

Will: 'I haven't been to the gym for quite a while and I'd like to get fit again. When I was at college I was dancing every other day so I do feel a bit unfit. I swim once a week at the moment, which is a bit bad. I normally run but I can't stand running in the winter.'

What are you going to buy with your first million?

Will: 'I'm going to get a new Mini! My first car was a Mini and I absolutely love them.'

You seem like an unlikely pop star …

Will: 'I knew this is what I wanted after I got through to the last fifty. I didn't want to do anything else but sing. I've been given a chance of a lifetime and I'm not going to waste it. I'm so determined to prove to the fans that I can make it to the best of my ability.'

Who would you most like to duet with?

Will: 'There are loads of people. I have to say James Brown is one of them. I'm a massive fan of Lauryn Hill's voice; I'd love to do something with her. I'd love to sing with Beth Orton too.'

Have you got any faults?

Will: 'I do. I'm quite forgetful. I'm quite bad at keeping in contact with people. Which is great now because I can use what I'm doing as an excuse. I can be quite selfish. Everyone has their faults. Oh, and smelly feet. I've got smelly feet. Fungus feet. My auntie gave me Odor-Eaters for Christmas. Which is really embarrassing.'

What's your main ambition?

Will: 'To remain happy.'

Press attention aside, it was time for Will to get on with the important job of rehearsing for the *Pop Idol Winner's Show*. He had new songs to learn, as well as an ITV interview with Kate Thornton to film. All this while trying to battle with a dodgy tummy that he'd picked up from somewhere, so he wasn't feeling his best.

Despite his grogginess, he perked up when he saw his fellow contestants during filming, and their reunion made him realize just how well they had all got on with each other throughout the difficult process of the competition. It also brought home to him how much he missed seeing them all on a regular basis, and how privileged he felt to have had the chance to take such a life-changing journey with them all.

After plenty of rehearsals, the show was filmed and everyone had a great time – especially at the wrap party afterwards. The booze flowed and there was plenty of singing, but all good things must come to an end and it was soon time for everyone to say their goodbyes. The winner's show marked the official end of the televised side of that incredible original series of *Pop Idol* – the first ever in what would go on to become a globally successful format. After this, a new chapter in Will's life would begin.

There were a few tears shed when all the contestants had to go their separate ways, but they walked away safe in the knowledge that they would soon be spending plenty more quality time with each other on the upcoming *Pop Idol* tour.

However, their sad and swift parting got Will thinking. He was worried that his busy new lifestyle would mean that he wouldn't have as much time as before to keep in touch with all of his friends and family – but he was determined to find a way. He made an effort to spend as much time as possible with Mary and their other friends, just hanging out at Mary's flat, but he also resigned himself to the fact that having downtime like this to catch up with mates could soon be a thing of the past. 'I may as well make the most of my time here, because I have a horrible feeling I might not be around much in the future,' he said.

He wasn't wrong. His diary was soon packed with meetings and important appointments. There were more photo shoots to do for his first single, and a meeting with *Pop Idol* judge Nicki Chapman and executive producer Simon Fuller, both from Will's new management company, 19.

In joining 19, Will was signing up to a company which looked after an impressive stable of high-profile, international stars, each more commercially successful than the next. Simon Fuller had set up the company back in 1985. 19 Management was quickly established as an entertainment company which looked after the interests of a number of prominent artists. Fuller personally masterminded the launch of the Spice Girls – the biggest girl group of all time – as well as looking after the careers of such diverse singers as Rachel Stevens and Annie Lennox, both of whose interests he still shepherds to this day.

The Spice Girls proved to be 19's first big success story. Fuller achieved worldwide domination with them in the mid-nineties, which helped to get him noticed on a grand scale. The girls themselves first got together in 1993, after answering an advert in the *Stage* magazine. They spent their early days playing small gigs in a bid to make a name for themselves and struggled to make ends meet, signing on the dole to pay the rent. It wasn't until 1995 that they signed a deal with Virgin Records and it looked like their dreams of stardom were finally going to come true.

But although the record deal changed everything, having sacked their old manager, they were now furiously on the lookout for a new one. At the end of 1995 they met Fuller, and decided that he was the man who could take them all the way to the top. It proved to be an astute move.

During their time together the group scored a massive nine number one singles and one number two hit, a trail-blazing record of success which began with 1996's summer anthem 'Wannabe'. The track instantly propelled the girls to worldwide celebrity when it became a hit across Europe and in the US: it hit number one in the States in January 1997. The Spice Girls were one of the few British bands of recent years to break America, and they spent a considerable amount of time touring the US throughout 1997, laying the foundations for what was already turning out to be a phenomenally successful career.

The five-piece also released three albums in their time together – *Spice*, *SpiceWorld* and *Forever* – but when they sacked Simon Fuller at the end of 1997, after deciding that they were capable of managing themselves, it signalled the beginning of the end for the girl group.

The ensemble eventually disbanded in 2000, having seen an increasing dip in their popularity following Geri's defection from the band in May 1998. All five girls then launched solo careers – with varying levels of success. Emma Bunton, who is now managed once again by Fuller, has released two Top Ten albums – 2001's *A Girl Like Me* and 2004's *Free Me*. Victoria 'Posh Spice' Beckham, who these days is best known for being the glamorous wife of footballer David Beckham, has also signed back up with Fuller, in a well-publicized deal which saw the manager take control of 'brand Beckham', with both husband and wife now signed to his books. Interestingly, it was Fuller who introduced the pair back in the late nineties – could he have foreseen the incredible financial clout that the marriage of two such celebrities would create? Victoria has tried (and sadly failed) to launch a solo singing career several times, and has released one album to date – 2001's self-titled number ten hit. It remains to be seen whether Fuller will put all the power of 19 behind Mrs Beckham to improve her musical fortunes, or whether he will opt to take his world-famous client down another route. For David, he has already negotiated several high-profile sponsorship deals, including agreements with Adidas, Pepsi and the 2004 mega-deal with Gillette razors, rumoured to be worth around $10 million.

As for the other Spices, Melanie B has released two albums over a five-year period – 2000's *Hot* and 2005's *LA State of Mind* – and is now living in LA with her young daughter, Phoenix Chi, where she is busy carving out an acting career for herself. Melanie C is considered to be the most successful ex-Spice Girl, having had three hit albums (*Northern Star*, *Reason* and *Beautiful Intentions*), and she is also seen as the most credible Spice by the music industry. Geri Halliwell, meanwhile, equals Mel C's tally of three albums with *Schizophonic*, *Scream If You Wanna Go Faster* and *Passion*, but the latter regrettably didn't afford her a great deal of success, charting at number forty-one. No matter what the status of their solo careers, though, all five girls have earned their place in musical history – and the input Fuller had into their early careers is indisputed.

Moreover, the success of the Spice Girls certainly wasn't a one-off. 19 Management has been responsible for 281 Top Forty albums and 430 Top Forty singles so far, officially making Fuller the most successful manager of all time.

And the scope of 19 doesn't just extend to the music industry. Fuller has expanded into the lucrative world of TV, too. It was he who came up with the *Pop Idol* concept – and as a result of the format being sold around the world it has made him an extremely wealthy man. In March 2005 he sold 19 Management to American billionaire Robert Sillerman for £200 million, so it's safe to say he could get away with putting his feet up for a while.

But in March 2002, there were more pressing matters at hand. In Will Young, Fuller had found himself an artist of enormous talent – but also one blessed with intelligence and drive. Will wanted to be very hands-on in his career, and at that first meeting with his new management – riding high on his recent wave of success – Will was determined to be in control from the word go, no matter what the illustrious reputation of the man sat in front of him. After all, Will had plenty he wanted to discuss with 19 – and one thing in particular had been playing on his mind. He was aware that things had been very rushed for previous TV-talent-show winners Hear'Say, after their *Popstars* victory, and he didn't want to go down the same route of throwing together an album that maybe wasn't up to standard, just because it would sell bucketloads off the back of the TV show if it was released quickly. Music was incredibly important in Will's life, and he was in this for the long run, so he wanted his debut album to be well crafted and worth people's hard-earned cash.

But both Simon and Nicki put his mind at rest by assuring him that there were no plans to rush the album out. In addition, Will would get the opportunity to work with some brilliant people – both producers and songwriters – and also to write some tracks himself if that was what he wanted.

Will left the meeting on a high, knowing that he and his prestigious new management company were on the same wavelength. 'I think I'm going to be very happy. I trust them completely because we have very similar ideas,' he said.

Will was lucky to be able to have such a big say in his future from the very beginning – something which is practically unheard of with new artists. He was well respected and his ideas were taken seriously from day one – indeed, to this day he still prides himself on the fact that no big decisions are made without his say so. From the off, Will set out as he meant to go on.

The Pop Idol's debut single, 'Evergreen'/'Anything Is Possible', was released on Monday 25 February. There were massive expectations for it after the incredible success of Hear'Say's debut offering the previous year – their first single smashed sales records by shifting 0.55 million copies in a week – but Will didn't let the pressure get to him. He wanted to enjoy the buzz of his first release and, apart from anything, he was far too busy to stress.

For at the start of that week, Will jetted off to Dublin, where he began working with producers at the famous Windmill Lane Studios on songs for his debut album. As well as being very productive creatively, the trip also gave him a chance to step out of the limelight for a couple of days. But that didn't mean there wasn't time for a little bit of partying while he was there. Will hit U2's hip nightclub The Kitchen, where he danced the night away in the VIP area and chatted politely with a number of admirers. One onlooker commented afterwards, 'He was surrounded by people all the time but was really polite and stopped to chat to everyone. He seemed to be having a great time and was laughing a lot, and also dancing whenever he got the chance. He's obviously enjoying his new pop-star life.'

The day after the double A-sided single was released, Will heard the news that it had sold over 300,000 copies on its first day, meaning that unless something dramatic happened in the meantime, it would be a sure-fire number one hit the following Sunday.

When at last Sunday came, Will headed down to the Pepsi Chart HQ to be interviewed by Dr Fox. He arrived to find that Leicester Square had been sectioned off especially for him. Will mania was getting more frenzied by the day.

That week's Top Five singles were counted down: 5. Nickelback – 'How You Remind Me'. 4. Lasgo – 'Something'. 3. Enrique Iglesias – 'Hero'. 2. Shakira – 'Whenever, Wherever'. Meaning that at number one was a former politics student who had taken a chance on fame and had just achieved his dream.

Will was handed an envelope by Foxy: inside was a piece of paper which would tell him how many singles he had sold that week. Will's hands trembled as he opened it up and read the mind-blowing figure out on air, revealing that his debut offering had shifted 1,108,659 copies in a single week, beating the previous record held by Band Aid's 1984 hit 'Do They Know It's Christmas?', and earning Will a place in the *Guinness Book of Records* into the bargain. He was presented with a Guinness Book Of Records plaque, which read: 'Presented to Will Young to celebrate the Pepsi Chart Number

One "Anything Is Possible"/"Evergreen" and on becoming the fastest-selling debut of all time.'

'Never in my wildest dreams did I think it would sell this many. It's unbelievable!' said a jubilant Will.

The next day Will was presented with another disc to celebrate the tracks going triple platinum, and later that week he filmed his first ever *Top of the Pops*. But his appearance on the show wasn't without its problems.

BMG, Will's record company, were determined that their star would sing both the singles on the show, but *TOTP* bosses wanted Will to sing only one song – and they weren't budging. The show's producer, Michael Kelpie, said at the time: 'The door is still open and we would be delighted to have Will on the show, but the record company and Simon Fuller have got to drop their unreasonable demands.'

Meanwhile, Pete Waterman threw his opinion into the mix, stating: 'I would've let him do one song. I think his management will find it great publicity, but I think his management are naive to ask the BBC to change their rules of a lifetime to do two tracks. Next the artist will want three tracks and then four tracks and, in fact, why don't you have us on the whole of *Top of the Pops* because we've got a greatest hits out.'

BMG told *Top of the Pops* that either Will got to sing both singles, or he wouldn't appear at all, but in the end a compromise was reached: *Top of the Pops* would begin screening the video to 'Evergreen' once Will's chart-topping position had been announced – but then the singer would appear in person to perform 'Anything Is Possible'. Will was delighted to be able to fulfil something which is every pop star's dream – appearing on the longest-running music show in the UK. 'I love doing *Top of the Pops*. It's what I've grown up with. It's such an institution,' Will said excitedly.

Will went on to stay at number one for a further two weeks, and was eventually knocked off the top spot by Gareth Gates's cover of 'Unchained Melody'. While Gareth's 900,000 first-week sales may not have beaten Will's 1.1 million, he still managed to make it into the record books as well, when – at age seventeen – he became the youngest British male solo star ever to have a number one single.

But Gareth's swift rise to glory – his own number one singles and record-breaking achievements – coming so soon after Will's success, got people speculating as to whether Gareth was being favoured over Will. Questions were asked as to why his single was released so soon after Will's, and why he seemed to be getting preferential treatment from the record company. Fuel was added to the already smouldering fire with Simon Cowell's open admission that he had wanted Gareth to win *Pop Idol*. Part of the problem was that Will and Gareth were with the same record company, BMG. But the pair were also linked through their management teams – both singers signed to 19 Management directly after the TV show finished. As the winner, Will was already guaranteed a deal with the highly regarded company. But Simon Fuller also chose to represent Will's fellow *Pop Idol* competitors Gareth and Zoe Birkett, the latter of whom went on to release one single, 2003's 'Treat Me Like A Lady'. The multiple signings caused mutterings of unfairness throughout the entertainment industry, and among fans. It was felt that the other deals took away the glory of Will being the overall winner, as a lot of attention was now also focused on Gareth.

As a management company, 19's job was to ensure that Will and Gareth's interests were taken care of with regard to sponsorship deals, press coverage and single and album releases. BMG was also heavily involved in these areas, and all decisions made about both their careers were a result of meetings between 19, BMG and the singers themselves. But almost immediately, fans sensed a difference in the way the rising stars were being treated.

For Gareth and Will were marketed very differently when they were launched to the public. While Gareth was aimed almost exclusively at a teen audience, Will was pitched slightly older – but he still managed to appeal to almost all age groups, from kids to grannies. Yet although it was Will who had the broader appeal, it was Gareth who landed the lucrative sponsorship deals. Shortly after *Pop Idol* ended, Gareth signed deals worth around £1 million with Wella hair products and Pepsi. Will didn't appear to have the same kinds of offers flooding in. Whether the proposals were on the table and he turned them down for fear of 'selling out' is not known, but people began to compare the pair's competing careers to the Liberty X/Hear'Say situation, where even though Liberty X were the runners-up in the *Popstars* competition, it was they who actually ended up coming out on top in the long run, after Hear'Say's short-lived success failed to stay the course.

There was further rivalry on the publishing front, too, when Will and Gareth's first books were unleashed to the public. Will's book, *Anything is Possible*, was up against Gareth's *Right From the Start* – and, predictably at that time, Will's book came off worse in the sales stakes. While the official Pop Idol's book sold an impressive 100,000 copies, Gareth's sold more than double that figure, around 250,000 copies. Newspaper articles speculated noisily about whether Gareth would actually turn out to be the true winner of *Pop Idol* commercially, but Will rose above it and got on with doing his new job as well as he could.

A former production manager at Will's publisher Contender Books, who worked with the star on both *Anything is Possible* and Will's second book, *By Public Demand*, is convinced that Will and his team were never troubled by Gareth's initial run of success. She comments, 'Gareth's book may have sold more, but I always got the feeling that 19 Management saw Will as more of a long player. Will was also very clever and you sensed that he didn't do anything that he didn't want to. Gareth seemed far more pliable. If we had a meeting with 19 Management, they would often look at each other when we suggested things for the Will book, as they were unsure about whether Will would agree to it. I think he was probably a little more difficult than they expected him to be and really knew his own mind.' And she concludes, 'Gareth's book may have done better, but Will's the one that's lasted so he's had the last laugh, really.'

Meanwhile, back in 2002, both lads got the chance to be album artists of sorts, when *Pop Idol: The Big Band Album* was released on 8 April. The collection featured all ten *Pop Idol* finalists singing thirteen of their favourite swing songs from the show, backed by noted orchestra The Big Blue. Will's contributions were 'Beyond The Sea' and 'I Won't Dance'. It would be several more months before the public got the chance to get their hands on Will's debut solo album, but this certainly kept them happy in the meantime.

CHAPTER SIX

That Thing Called Love

When you're the hottest new pop star on the block, there are certain things that are expected of you. To be talented, to be good-looking, and to appeal to teenage girls who are going to buy your records – namely by appearing single and available to them – are just three of the requirements. It's primarily down to this latter aspect of the job that singers such as George Michael and Boyzone's Stephen Gately hid the fact that they were gay from their fans for many years. It's not that they themselves didn't want to come out, but there is often pressure from record-company executives for stars to keep their homosexuality a secret, in a bid to sell more singles or albums.

There were already murmurings about Will's sexuality during *Pop Idol*. But while it was no secret to those close to him that he was gay, Will didn't feel ready to reveal such a private thing to the world at large in those early days.

It was obvious, though, that even then Will's popularity spanned all age groups – 'I get fan mail from six-year-old girls to sixty-five-year-old aunties. It's amazing!' he exclaimed at the time – so it was unlikely that his coming out would have stopped people voting for him week after week. But that didn't mean that he was about to start shouting about his sexuality from the rooftops.

Will first spoke to his press officer about the fact that he was gay during the pre-live-show rehearsals. He was concerned about it coming out in the newspapers before he was ready and equipped for it to do so, and he wanted to get her advice. 'I was worried in case somebody asked about my sexuality, because at that point I wasn't comfortable talking about it. It was on my mind, certainly. I talked about the whole issue to the people at *Pop Idol*. The truth is I just didn't want any stories appearing in the papers about my sexuality during the show, mainly because it was totally irrelevant. The show was about my singing and I didn't want to find myself in papers because it would have put me in the spotlight above the others – that wouldn't have been fair. In the end, nothing appeared to take the viewers' minds off my singing abilities.'

Fairness in the competition aside, however, Will is notoriously private when it comes to his relationships and he wanted to choose when was the right time to tell people. It was such a personal thing for him, and therefore not a decision he wanted to take lightly. 'It's one thing telling your friends and family that you're gay, but it's slightly daunting imagining it written in the press when I've never been in a national newspaper in my life,' Will admitted at the time.

Needless to say, during his time in *Pop Idol* the press were always trying to find out information about Will's personal life and often probed him on his relationship status – as they did with all the other contestants. There is always a huge battle between different newspapers to break the biggest stories on celebrities, and with *Pop Idol* one of the most watched shows on TV (and its stars' lives fresh fodder for the tabloids), the race was on to uncover any *Pop Idol* scandal that the hacks could find.

One newspaper in particular was desperately trying to out Will and kept making pointed comments whenever they wrote about him. Will said: 'There was one thing in [one of the tabloid papers] that was pretty nasty, and it did hurt. They tried to make out I was in some kind of homosexual fighting club, which is just nonsense. But it was all so badly written. As the article progressed the writer started saying things like "and he's really ugly" and "his hair is a mess". In the end I had to laugh. It was pathetic.'

But Mr Young was always far too savvy to slip up, even when, during a press conference, a journalist posed the question of who his dream date would be. Will, already a master at deflecting difficult questions, replied that he would like to 'have tea with the Queen'. And when another asked which of his fellow contestants he fancied most, he replied diplomatically, 'Erm, wow, I haven't really thought about it. Can I say none?'

However, in March 2002 – just weeks after *Pop Idol* reached its dramatic finale – Will finally felt that it was time to reveal to the public that he was gay. He had discovered that some guy, a man Will didn't even know, was hawking a story around the papers that they had slept together. It seemed it was only a matter of time before someone did some kind of exposé on the newly crowned victor, and Will decided that if the papers were going to print that he was gay, he wanted to be a part of it and have some control over what was said.

He spoke to Sunday newspaper the *News of the World*, telling them: 'I feel it's time to tell my fans I'm gay. It's totally no big deal, just part of who I am. For me it's normal and nothing to be ashamed about. I'm gay and I'm comfortable with that. I really don't know what the fuss is about. I always try to be honest with myself and truthful with everyone.'

He admitted that he was certain most people had already guessed he was gay, so it wouldn't be a huge shock to them.

'I'm sure this will not come as a surprise to many people, although I've always been discreet and I'm not a campaigner when it comes to my sexuality.'

Will said that his decision to tell the world he was gay largely came about because he felt pressure from certain quarters of the media, but he stressed that it wasn't an issue as far as family, friends and work went. He explained, 'Some other media pressure has led me to talk about my private life. My family and friends have known ever since I have. They've always been there for me. And my management have been fantastic. I had a long conversation with the boss Simon Fuller … and told him about my decision to come out publicly. He was totally relaxed and supportive and left it up to me to decide when, or if, I wanted to talk about it. Now is that time.'

Ex-*Pop Idol* judge Simon Cowell made a statement about Will's decision, saying that he thought Will was brave to speak out. 'He probably felt it was better to get it out in the open rather than keeping it bottled up,' Simon said. 'To tell you the truth, I couldn't give a toss. We obviously had an inkling that Will was gay. It was a bit of a giveaway when he was asked about his ideal date and he said he wanted to have dinner with the Queen. When stories began circulating, he and Simon [Fuller] made a decision that it was appropriate to put his side of the story. I think it is very brave.'

Meanwhile, George Michael commented, 'It didn't come as a surprise to me but I'm impressed that he did it. It was fairly obvious though.'

Will later reflected on his decision to come out, and knew without a doubt that he'd made the right choice. 'Maybe people like George Michael and Elton John have paved the way and made it a little easier for someone like me. My take on it was to just say it, get it out of the way and move on. I remember thinking at the time that, if my career plummeted as a result, then I didn't want to be a part of it anyway. I would have gone and worked in a dog refuge or something.'

Will also divulged that, contrary to popular opinion, his team were one hundred per cent behind his decision. 'To be honest, everyone thought the people around me were trying to stop me revealing the truth, but that's not so,' he said. And he continued, 'I was very pleased with the response. It's not affected me at all [career-wise]. I've still got a lot of female fans. [In fact,] the whole gay thing has been fantastic. There's been nothing but support for me from my record label and my family ever since I came out. It's been really positive. So for me, nothing's really changed.'

After all, as Will himself points out, he had already gone through the stress of coming out a few years before, so deciding to make a public statement about his sexuality really wasn't a huge thing for him to have to deal with. It simply meant that another aspect of his life was revealed to the public. Will jokes, 'It was a bit like, "Hey, Will, what did you do Sunday?" "Oh, I came out in the papers, and then I went to the studio to write a song." I mean, come on, there are more important stories than my sexuality.'

And he was delighted by the response he got from fans. 'I have had such lovely letters – from eighty-year-olds to twelve-year-olds – all wishing me well. It's quite incredible,' he said. 'The fact that I've had so many nice letters and cards says it all for me, really. The news came out just before the *Pop Idol* tour, and I think the concerts helped me in terms of support. The crowds were just amazing. I got such a warm response from them. I think the tour also helped everyone else focus back on my music and not on my private life. When I'm out and about, people have stopped to say hello or good luck. It's amazing. In my statement to the press I said, "Yes, I'm gay, now let me get on with my music career." And that's what I want to do.'

Will's coming out touched some people deeply, as he discovered when a young man approached him in a pub shortly after the interview was published, wanting to let Will know how much he had affected his life. Will recalls, 'One of the best things that happened to me after coming out in the papers was when this chap came up to me in a pub and said, "I saw you had come out in the papers and now I've just come out to my family. Thanks for being so honest." I thought that was amazing because if I could help one person then it's been worth it.'

But even with the issue of his sexuality cleared up, press interest in Will's personal life was still strong. Not that Will was overly concerned about any potential exposés. When asked if he was worried about any kiss-and-tells coming out in the tabloids, he joked: 'It's not a worry. Not unless my dog could talk, because I always kiss my dog before I go to bed.'

When it comes to love, Will reckons he's never had a disastrous date because, 'I don't really go on dates. I tend to get to know people first as friends.' He describes his best date ever as the time that he 'once went to Cornwall with somebody for the weekend and we spent our time hanging out on the beach. It was lovely.'

Will confesses that he is a complete romantic and has total faith that he will meet the love of his life at some point in the future. He's a believer in love at first sight. 'I think one day I'll see someone across the room and go, "Yes, that's the person,"' he says confidently. And he certainly isn't one to settle for second best. 'I think you should be with someone who makes you happy, and challenges you, and brings out a good side to your character,' he explains. 'Because I haven't ever had a relationship, in terms of having a boyfriend, I look at friends' relationships and it seems to me that a lot of them are with people who don't make them that happy. I think there's an urge to be with someone that seems to override people's thoughts of their own well-being. People think of it as failure, but it isn't at all. There's a friend of mine who's got loads of personality, is really gorgeous-looking, perfect boyfriend material, who doesn't have a girlfriend. He's never had a relationship, and he's just so cool about it, and I think that's really attractive. I might worry I had commitment problems if I was thirty-five and still single, but at the moment I'm fairly chilled.'

After Will came out, people speculated that it was because he had a secret boyfriend and he wanted to be upfront about it. However, a friend of the star revealed, 'He's only ever had two close relationships and is now really too busy to have a partner. He's totally focused on his career at the moment.'

Will himself commented: 'My love life could be better! But I think if you're a driven person there's always something that falls by the wayside. I'm a little busy for love at the mo and I'm also rubbish at chatting people up. I always end up saying something like, "Cotton wool, it's really underrated, don't you think?" It's definitely something I need to work on.'

Will admits to having a huge crush on David Beckham and has said in the past: 'I would even sing with Posh to get close to David – he's my ideal man.' But fantasies aside, what's the deal with Will's real-life love affairs?

In August 2002 two newspapers printed stories claiming that Will was desperate to find love. But when asked if the stories were true – was he frantically trying to find a man? – he laughed and said, 'No, not really. I wouldn't believe some of the things that are in the papers. [But] if and when I do have a boyfriend, you won't see us in matching his 'n' hers towelling dressing gowns, doing "At home" spreads in the glossies.'

And the fiercely private star is true to his word. Since

Will's revelation about being gay, he's always done his utmost to keep his personal life as much under wraps as possible. He claims that his love life is non-existent and he has been single – on and off – for some time.

But being single doesn't exclude the possibility of dates, and Will has in fact been linked with several guys since he became famous, including a ballet dancer called Steve Brown, whom he met at the BRITs in 2003, and Andrew Kinlochan from boy band Phixx. However, there has never been any confirmation that Will dated either of them and he remains tight-lipped about his romances.

'I haven't met the right person,' Will confided recently. 'Lots of my closest friends haven't had relationships but that doesn't mean they're monks. The truth is, I have no wish to talk about past relationships, which people claim have or haven't happened. I've said this all along because I feel quite strongly about this. I am aware of the media interest in my life, but I do have a right to privacy. I cannot speculate on what will happen or what I will do if I do meet anyone. But I'm sure I'll cope.'

In 2004 Will was also linked to a professional footballer, who had a long-term girlfriend. But the singer was quick to dismiss the gossip. 'It's an every-week occurrence with me; that poor guy probably hates me,' Will said of the untrue rumours.

As for some of the other ridiculous stories? How about the one that he was dating Emma Bunton? 'No. We're good friends though,' Will laughs. And the gossip about Christina Aguilera lusting after him? 'I quite like that idea. I thought that was terrifying, but it's great. Maybe [she just hasn't] got the message or something. Maybe it's that untouchable thing,' he says.

There was one ongoing rumour that turned out to be true, however. But sadly it didn't mean that Will had met his Mr Right. It transpired that Will dated fashion designer Matthew

Williamson for a time. The pair were first linked in 2004, but it was only in August 2005 that Matthew finally admitted that they had enjoyed more than simple friendship together. 'I was seeing him for a while and now we're great friends,' Matthew told style magazine *Elle*.

So for Will, the search for love continues ... but with so much on his plate career-wise, he's hardly pining away. As it is, it's a wonder he's had time even to stop to take a breath – let alone a chance on romance – since those early, hectic days at the start of 2002.

CHAPTER SEVEN

Hitting The Road And A Royal Engagement

The beginning of March 2002 saw rehearsals begin for the upcoming *Pop Idol* arena tour, which would take the final ten contestants around the country for an impressive twenty-one gigs. It was the perfect opportunity for the final ten to spend some quality time together and have a proper catch-up after the madness of the past couple of weeks.

The show was a sell-out – 18,000 tickets for the two opening nights at Wembley Arena sold out in just two-and-a-half hours. Thousands of fans would be making the journey to see their Pop Idols in all their glory night after night, so it had to be a top-class show – and there was a lot of work to be done.

Even though the finalists had already had extensive training on *Pop Idol* itself, more vocal and dance training was essential as it was the first time the final ten would be performing in a proper tour. As they would be singing continuously, they needed to learn how to look after their voices, so they could make it through the gruelling schedule and still be able to sing in their usual fantastic fashion by the end of the run.

Will vowed to stay off booze for a while, to make sure that his vocal chords were in good shape for the shows. 'I just can't drink any more for a while. I've overdone it,' Will admitted, 'especially after filming my video in Cuba. I went on a huge bender there, and I've been on a few more since.'

The vocal preparation and dance rehearsals took place in three different venues – a London hotel, the LWT studios in Brixton, and a huge studio that closely resembled the arenas they would be gracing, so that the singers could get used to the feel of such large spaces. TV studios may look huge on the small screen, but in real life they're fairly compact, so the massive arenas were going to take some getting used to.

Will was excited about embarking on his first ever tour and said: 'I can't wait to get back on stage and start performing again. I'm really looking forward to being out there with the fans. I'm determined to give them a great show. I just love being up there on stage. That's when I'm happiest.'

The tour kicked off on 14 March 2002 at London's Wembley Arena. Will opened the show with 'Light My Fire', and being up on stage again made him realize that all the hard work of the past six months had been more than worth it. He was finally getting to do what he'd always dreamed of – entertaining the masses in huge venues across the country. 'I've been so excited about it! I can't wait to see the audiences and just perform for them, because up until now we've always been auditioning. And I'm really looking forward to being with the other nine guys, because we had such a laugh together during the TV series,' he said. 'It's going to be the most amazing feeling in the world. Going on stage is like surfing a huge wave. This huge sound from the crowd suddenly hits you, the adrenalin starts pumping and you just get carried away by your performance. It's incredible. I always get really nervous before performing and am always paranoid about tripping up. If there are any steps involved, you can guarantee I'll slip up.'

Thankfully, however, he managed to remain slip-free throughout the tour. Instead, each night Will closed the show to massive applause, leaving no one in any doubt as to who the true star of the show was. But, ever-modest, Will made sure that he gave his fellow crooners their dues and paid his respects to their talents whenever he got the chance. All ten performers got on brilliantly. 'The tour really cemented my friendship with people like Jess, who I didn't know as well as Zoe and Hayley, and we got on so well,' Will remembers fondly.

When asked with whom he got on best out of his touring partners, Will replied: 'I love all of them for different reasons. I think it's like you have different friends for different sides of your character. I mean, I would say Gareth because we were there right to the end. Hayley and I, obviously everyone knows we got on very well. We did the duet together [on the *Pop Idol Winner's Show* and on the tour]. And Jessica is just the loveliest girl in the world. I love all of them for different reasons. But those three particularly. And Zoe. They really stand out.'

Not surprisingly, everywhere the Pop Idols went they caused a massive stir. Not that Will was minding the attention – it just felt a bit weird every now and again. 'I don't look for the attention at all, but it's really flattering when it happens, because people have been so nice. This'll sound cheesy, but I think it's because all ten of us are kind of the people's people, the ones the public chose. And they feel that they know us, so it's great when they come up and say, "Well done." The weirdest thing was walking through the local supermarket and suddenly being confronted with a 30-foot poster of myself. That was slightly freaky. But quite fun as well.'

While the first half of the gig was dedicated to renditions

of popular hits by the final ten (with a performance of 'Evergreen' thrown in by Will to rapturous applause), the second half was all about big-band songs. Backed by a nineteen-strong band, Gareth put his own stamp on Weill and Brecht's 'Mack The Knife', Darius belted out the Nat King Cole classic 'Let There Be Love', while Will wowed the crowds yet again with his brilliant version of Charles Trenet's 'Beyond The Sea'.

It was a hectic schedule that involved non-stop travelling, and getting enough sleep was the one thing Will had been worried about on tour. 'It's not so much that I'm a party animal and have loads of late nights, but I do like my sleep. You can't beat a nice lie-in,' he said during the run-up to the tour.

But once it all kicked off, he found it didn't bother him at all. 'I don't mind travelling and I enjoy driving through the country with my Walkman on, staring out the window. Once you get over the first couple of nights, you get used to it and slip into a routine.'

And the *Pop Idol* gang even managed to slip in the odd night out … 'Birmingham was a mess. Three old friends from uni came up and stayed and we got wrecked. We ended up walking around the gardens at 4 a.m.,' Will confesses.

But he certainly paid for his raucous night out, and was suffering so much the next morning that he had to have a sleep on the tour bus to ensure that he was well enough to perform in Newcastle that night. Despite his forty winks, he still found the gig a bit of a struggle but was very proud that he managed to make it through the entire show without mishap.

It was a similar story when Will's family came up to stay with him after the Glasgow gig, where the crew held an official tour bash and everyone partied long into the night, with the Youngs being some of the last to go to bed. In the middle of the night, a screeching fire alarm went off, meaning that the hotel had to be evacuated. The only people who managed to sleep through the ruckus were, in the words of Will, 'the drunk Young men' – Will, his brother Rupert and their dad, Robin.

The tour came full circle when it arrived back in London on 6 April and the final ten played a concert at the London Arena in aid of the Prince's Trust. It was announced that Will, Gareth and Darius had been named as young ambassadors for the charity following their visit to a project in Tower Hamlets, east London. 'It is a huge honour and a fantastic opportunity for us to be able to fund-raise for such a great cause,' said Will. 'Because of *Pop Idol* and the success of the show, people feel like they know us. And it is a good way to use us to help the work of the Prince's charity.'

Using his newfound fame for positive reasons was something Will was discovering he could do often. Just the week before, the star had been called upon to make a plea for a missing Surrey teenager to get in touch with her worried family and friends. Will immediately agreed to assist.

Milly Dowler had been missing for eight days when Will made the appeal, a few hours before he went on stage in Sheffield. Milly was a huge fan of Will's, and had attended one of the *Pop Idol* concerts just days before her disappearance.

'Milly, you are not in trouble, your family and friends love you very much, and you are greatly missed,' Will said during the moving televised appeal. 'If you are watching, please simply call a friend or any family member to let them know you are safe.'

Tragically, Milly's body was found the following September in Yateley Heath Forest, near Fleet in Hampshire. Will was deeply touched by the tragedy, and in October 2003 he headlined a special gala event held to celebrate the life of the murdered teenager and to raise funds for the newly established Milly's Fund charity.

By the time the *Pop Idol* tour came to an end, in April 2002, the talented ten had performed to over 250,000 fans and received some rave reviews, with Will having praise heaped on him from every quarter. It was a great response to his first live shows. The BBC News website commented, 'The Pop Idol himself, Will Young, handled his performance and the audience with a pleasant, relaxed confidence, as he sang "Light My Fire", "Evergreen" and "Beyond The Sea",' while the *Guardian* reported, 'Young appears genuinely surprised by his ecstatic reception as he tears through "Light My Fire". He is perfectly suited to the big-band style that takes up the second half of the show.' Such positive feedback from such highly respected sources provided all the reassurance that Will might have needed to convince himself that he was here to stay in his new career. The reviews validated everything he had always aspired to, and had known in his heart that he could always achieve, given the opportunity.

Having worked harder than he ever had in his life over recent weeks, Will now headed to Italy on holiday, where he listened to music and read books and spent plenty of time in the company of close friends. He was still getting used to being recognized, so some time away from it all gave him a well-earned break and a chance to recharge his batteries.

All too soon, though, he was back in the thick of it. The Simon Cowell/Will Young battle was ignited once again when Simon made some fresh comments to the press about the pair's working relationship. Simon had been heavily involved in the earliest stages of Will's career, and had had a say in music releases and the direction that Will's career should take. However, due to his heavy work commitments with BMG, *Pop Idol* and *American Idol* (and the fact that it was no secret that Simon and Will didn't really get on), the music executive later took a step back from things with regard to Mr Young. But now the issue was flaring up again.

Simon agreed in part that the reason he was so much more involved with Gareth's career was because he and Will weren't on the best of terms, but had gone on record to deny that this meant he wanted Gareth to be more successful. 'I don't think Will wants to work with me and so I put my energies into Gareth,' he reasoned. 'I don't think Will likes me very much. Maybe I was nasty to him. The difference between Will and Gareth is that Gareth wants to work with me and take my ideas and I don't think Will does. I suggested something to Will recently and he said no. I told him he was making a mistake. I would love to work with Will more, but you can only do so much.

'I have more input into Gareth's career, whereas Will wants to do his own thing. Gareth is more willing to listen to my suggestions; he's a lot like Westlife in that respect. But Gareth and Will are very different people; they have their own opinions on things. But there isn't a conspiracy. I'm running a business and they're both on my label [Simon set up his own record label through BMG, S Records, in 2000 – both Will and Gareth are signed to it] and I would be stupid to favour one over the other. I want both of them to be successful.'

But it wasn't only Will that Simon was falling out with. The boss of 19 Management, Simon Fuller, had a bone to pick with Mr Cowell regarding the latter's new TV show, *The X Factor*, due to debut on screens in 2004. Though the pair had built an incredibly strong manager/record-company partnership through their mutual work on *Pop Idol* and *American Idol*, that all meant nothing when it came to business. Fuller accused his former friend and colleague of ripping off the *Pop Idol* format when Cowell created *The X Factor*. The TV branch of 19 Management filed a copyright infringement and breach of contract lawsuit against Simon and his production companies

Simco and Syco, as well as producer Fremantle Media. Currently (autumn 2005), the case is ongoing, but has never made it to court. However, at the beginning of the second series of *The X Factor* in August 2005, Fuller expressed his anger once again, causing Cowell to rant: 'Every time we announce a new show five people come out of the woodwork and say, "We had that idea." I've never ripped off another show in my life.'

But the bickering of the executives was still a long way off as Will faced his latest challenge: the release of his second single. With a huge buzz still surrounding Will's debut release three months on, he decided to wait until June to release his second offering – his jazzy take on The Doors' 'Light My Fire', which had gone down such a storm when he had performed it on *Pop Idol*. He described the track as 'quite a sexy song with a slightly Cuban feel', which made it the perfect track for the start of summer.

The B-side of the single boasted 'Ain't No Sunshine' and 'Beyond The Sea', both of which were firm favourites with fans when Will had showcased them during the competition.

The song was accompanied by a sexy black-and-white video which showed Will looking slicker than ever. The video was shot at Englefield House, a beautiful mansion in Berkshire. It was centred around a model called Fanny, whose performance was based on a famous sixties model called Edie Sedgwick. The video itself was loosely based on a black-and-white film called *Ciao! Manhattan*, from 1972.

The video was directed by Bailey Walsh, who had previously directed for the likes of Massive Attack and INXS, and Will knew he was the right person for the job the minute he saw his showreel. Unlike Will's debut videos, which had necessarily been devised and filmed on a tight schedule, due to the short time lapse between the singer winning *Pop Idol* and the announced release date of his first single, on the

'Light My Fire' video Will was able to be much more hands-on and take the time to get the shoot just right.

He and the crew had a brilliant time creating the arty video. Shortly after filming, when Will was asked in an interview what his biggest highlight since winning *Pop Idol* had been to date, he replied, 'The second day of the video for "Light My Fire". We had sack races and wheelbarrow races. I got very competitive and had to win them. And it was just an amazing day. It was really sunny and it was so much fun. It was just amazing. I said it was the highlight of my career. Because it was such a laugh, I think you can see it's all so natural. There was really no acting involved. We were having a laugh.'

Despite a great song and a killer video, Will has revealed that he was terrified about the single's release. With so much to live up to after the stunning success of his debut, it's little wonder that he was concerned about the reaction it would get from the record-buying public. Especially as he had some stiff competition in the form of his friends, *Pop Idol* hosts Ant and Dec, who were releasing their official World Cup single, 'On The Ball', on the same day.

Nevertheless, Will remained positive and said realistically that he didn't expect the same kind of sales from 'Light My Fire' that his debut had achieved. 'Any single that has six to eight months of PR behind it – riding on the top of the phenomenon that was *Pop Idol* – should sell well. Obviously I didn't know the sales were going to be that high, but they're bound to go down after that. I don't think that's a bad thing,' he said.

Then, of course, there was the stigma of releasing another cover version – something which did worry Will. 'It was one of those songs I did on the show which was a huge hit with the public. People hadn't really noticed me and then I came in with this very different song to what everyone else had done.

Then I talked back to Simon [Cowell], and all that was sort of shaped around "Light My Fire". It is a worry that it's another cover, but then I know what's coming up with the album. I suppose I think of the bigger picture.'

The other matter playing on Will's mind around this time was his smoking habit. He had recently given it up and was determined to beat the demon white sticks. 'I've decided enough is enough. It's a filthy habit. If anyone catches me doing it, I'll make a donation to the British Lung Foundation.

'The gym is helping me,' he revealed. 'I am really cross with myself. I haven't been smoking long. It was only when I went to university. Which is stupid because I managed to get through all the peer-pressure years. And then I started smoking. But it's horrible. I loathe it and I don't think anyone should do it. And it isn't good for your voice.'

Will soon discovered that when it came to his follow-up single, he had nothing to worry about. 'Light My Fire' knocked Eminem's 'Without Me' clean off the top spot, while Ant and Dec managed to chart at a respectable number three. 'Light My Fire' remained at number one for two weeks, selling in excess of 300,000 copies.

'I'd always dreamt of doing a version of this song and for it to get to number one is amazing,' Will said of his triumph. 'It was the song that got me noticed on *Pop Idol*, so it's special to me.' And in the flush of success, the nation's favourite singer didn't forget the people who had made it all happen. 'I want to say a massive thank you to everyone who went out and bought the single last week. I'm so happy that it's number one and it's just amazing. I can't really believe it, two number ones, it's quite astonishing. If it wasn't for all you guys going out and buying the music, then I wouldn't be here, so thank you so much and I'm really, really over the moon.'

And there were yet more great things to come. On Monday

3 June Will played at the Queen's Jubilee Concert at Buckingham Palace. Some time before, the organizers had approached Will about taking part, and he had immediately – and excitedly – accepted. As he remarked, 'One minute I'm joking about having tea with Her Majesty, and now I'm being invited to Buckingham Palace!'

In an interview with Sir David Frost just before the event, Will laughed: 'I tell you what, this time a year ago I would have just finished my exams, so I would have been sleeping in, probably not thinking about much else actually. [Now] I've never been so nervous, but I've never been so excited and it's very strange and I'm hoping that I can change that nervousness into excitement before I go on, otherwise I'm in a bit of trouble. But I'm very excited at the moment.'

At 3 p.m. on 3 June, a car arrived at his west London home to take him to the Queen's central London residence. The show was going to be watched by millions of people around the world, and would be Will's biggest gig to date, without question. Needless to say he was already feeling jumpy. He confided: 'It's just exciting and I want to soak the whole thing up. You know when it's somebody's wedding, or Christmas is coming, and you feel unlike any other time of the year because you're so excited the whole time? Well, this is how I've been feeling since rehearsals last week. It's not often you get to play at Buckingham Palace – for the Queen.'

After rigorous security checks Will and his small entourage were allowed into the palace gardens and Will immediately began his warm-up. That involved him listening to the songs he was going to be singing on stage later that day, and drinking copious amounts of herbal tea.

Leading music acts such as Tom Jones, Eric Clapton, Blue and The Corrs were also set to perform, and there were all sorts of rumours in the lead-up to the big show that Will would be duetting with Paul McCartney, Elton John or even Burt Bacharach. But, on the night, he flew solo with a spine-tingling rendition of Marvin Gaye's 'Heard It Through The Grapevine'. Sandwiched in between Atomic Kitten and Blue in the running order, Will wowed the 12,000-strong crowd who were lucky enough to have snared tickets for the momentous event in the palace gardens.

But that wasn't to be his only appearance that evening. He later joined the band Queen to sing 'We Are The Champions' – a role Phil Collins had suggested him for. Will said afterwards, 'It was absolutely petrifying during rehearsals, but on the night it was electric, absolutely electric.'

Will took to the stage for the final time during the finale, when all the day's performers joined together to sing The Beatles songs 'Hey Jude' and 'All You Need Is Love'. The Queen herself then appeared on stage and walked along the row of performers, which boasted some of the biggest musical artists in the world. She stopped to speak to Will, but the noise of the crowd was so deafening that he couldn't hear what she had said to him. 'All I caught was "...on TV," so I think she said, "I've seen you on TV." I couldn't really ask her to repeat what she'd said!' Will laughed afterwards.

The Pop Idol also exchanged a few words with Princes Charles and William, bringing what had been an extraordinary day and evening to an incredible end.

Will said of the once-in-a-lifetime event afterwards: 'It was pretty amazing and I was so star-struck with all these people around. There was Eric Clapton having a cup of tea, and Sir Paul McCartney. It was amazing. Singing with Queen was something I would never have dreamt of doing. It was quite a challenge, but I think it went quite well. I don't know, I woke up the next morning and thought, "What the hell did I do last night?" It was all a bit bizarre.'

Will took a well-earned break following the concert and headed to Cannes in the South of France with his family. The crushing pressure of the past few months was taking its toll. He felt that he was constantly talking about himself, and needed to have some time to get perspective on things before the next, inevitable round of interviews and TV appearances began. As Will had always been the kind of guy who would happily sit for hours listening to others talking, suddenly to be on the receiving end of all the attention all of the time came as a real shock. Wherever he went he was always under the microscope, and thanks to *Pop Idol* the public almost felt like they owned a little piece of him, and a lot was expected from him at all times. Because of this, he and his management always made sure that he took regular breaks so that he didn't get burnt out – something which is all too common in the music industry.

While he was on holiday, Will found an uninvited guest in his bedroom. But it wasn't an over-amorous fan or a lost cleaning lady – it was something altogether spookier.

Late one night, he woke suddenly and instantly became aware of a weird noise, like someone saying 'Why? Why? Why?' in his ear, and the sound of someone stamping on the floor. Terrified, Will got out of bed and looked out of the window. At this point, he saw a black figure run past. It was then that he suspected that a ghost had left the room. A very shaken Will eventually went back to bed and tried to get some sleep. Of course, people are often sceptical about ghostly experiences after the event, and the next morning Will began to question whether or not he had *really* seen anything. But then his brother Rupert, who was staying in the room next door, admitted that he'd had exactly the same experience during their stay, and that confirmed Will's suspicions that they weren't the only ones occupying the old building.

Ghostly experiences notwithstanding, the holiday was soon over, and after returning from his break Will spent much of the summer playing huge roadshows around the country. There was also one very special gig. Will had clearly made a lasting impression on the royals during the Queen's Jubilee Concert, for at the end of June he got the chance to perform for royalty again, when he played at an exclusive secret concert for 200 VIPs at Prince Charles's country retreat, Highgrove, in Gloucestershire.

Will treated the guests, including Prince Charles, Camilla Parker Bowles and Princes William and Harry, to renditions of old-time swing tracks at the bash, which was in aid of the British Forces Foundation. He was the only performer on the night and had been hand-picked to entertain everyone. Less than six months after he released his first single, Will Young was quite literally performing 'by royal appointment'. It was a remarkable achievement.

The young singer also headed to Dublin around this time, to continue work on his album with esteemed producers Richard Stannard and Julian Gallagher, alias Biff and Jules, who have worked with everyone from the Spice Girls to Gabrielle. Will was impressed by their accomplished music pedigree, while they were equally wowed by Will's talents. 'There are very few young artists who, when we record them, sing through the whole song,' says Biff. 'You tend to do the verse, then the chorus, and piece the whole thing together. But he sings it all. The only other artists we work with who do that are Gabrielle and Bono.'

High praise indeed. Will learnt a lot from the legendary producers and admits that he was rather green about the whole recording process before his trips to Dublin. But being in their company opened his eyes to new songwriting methods and he was soon on a roll, scribbling down ideas ten to the dozen. 'I can tinkle away on the piano a bit, but when I'm co-writing I need to get with people who have great grooves, because essentially I'm a melody-and-lyric man. If you've got a groove, the rest will come!' he enthused.

Will loved spending time in Dublin as no one batted an eyelid when they spotted their famous visitor. 'It's really nice to get over to Ireland. Dublin's such a wonderful place and they're very chilled out over there, you know. I wander around and it's absolutely no problem. I think they're probably used to a lot of stars being over there and they're just really friendly people and it is an atmosphere that is quite conducive to work. So it's really quite fun to be over there.'

With his debut album release just around the corner, Will's revived work ethic and Irish inspiration were perfectly timed. As the world eagerly anticipated the first LP from Britain's hottest star, Will knuckled down to yet more hard graft.

CHAPTER EIGHT

A Party In The Park And
A Debut Album

As the summer of 2002 hotted up, Will's debut album became his main focus. It was scheduled for release in the autumn and he was desperate for it to fulfil everyone's expectations. 'I think it's going to be very nerve-racking when the album comes out, because you don't know how people are going to take it. But I'm so pleased with it, and I can't wait,' he said.

Will made no secret of the fact that one of the things that was most important to him about the first album was getting the chance to write his own songs. And he got his wish. 'I'd never done any songwriting – I've always wanted to write songs but I never knew how to go about it,' he said during the recording of the album. 'I play the piano but not well enough to write music. I used to record melodies and record my voice but I never had any instruments – it's been such a great learning experience. It's really nice to be involved in the whole writing process, because that's what I'm gaining confidence in, as a writer. The latest song I've written is very European, slightly harking back to the sixties. It's cheesy but more tongue-in-cheek than real cheese – one to listen to in a rowing boat, floating down a river. It's lovely. One of my aims for the future is to keep on writing. To really get into my writing.'

Despite his enthusiasm for penning his own tunes, however, Will was also happy to record other people's tracks and had the attitude that if a single was good, it was good whoever wrote it. 'I think it's very important that you get the right songs. If someone comes to me with a great song then I'll sing it. If I happen to write it and it's brilliant then I'll sing that as well. I definitely want to write more because I love the creative process, but I'm quite happy to sing great songs wherever they come from. I think sometimes there's a lot of stress to write your own songs. I just enjoy singing, it doesn't matter – any time, any place!'

As well as working with Biff and Jules, Will also worked a great deal with Cathy Dennis, a former eighties pop star who has penned numerous global hits, including Kylie Minogue's colossal smash 'Can't Get You Out Of My Head'. Her impressive CV confirms her status as the most successful British female songwriter of the past three decades. Incidentally, Cathy's manager is also Simon Fuller, and the two 19 artists formed a productive partnership for Will's debut release.

Ms Dennis also joined forces with musical legend Burt Bacharach to write the ballad 'What's In Goodbye' for Will. 'I think it is a really pretty song. Cathy Dennis wrote beautiful lyrics and Will sounds marvellous on it,' Burt said of the track, and he was clearly already a fan of Mr Young. 'I like his voice. I heard the record and he sounds like a dream on it. I think the pressure is huge and he has got a freshness about him, he's got exuberance about him. I think he has a quality and he is a very handsome young man and he is excited about life and excited about the business and there is nothing that feels jaded about him. And I hope he never becomes jaded.'

Will described the as-yet-untitled album as 'really varied' and revealed that there were pop, jazz and slower-paced songs to be found on it. 'On the album there will be plenty of original, self-written and co-written material. I know there's a huge demand from my fans to hear some original Will songs, which is hugely flattering, and I am as keen to get them released as everyone else is. I just want to make sure that when I do release them, I am really proud of them,' he said.

Moreover, as well as original songs, Will was keen to include some of the covers he had performed endlessly over the past few months. 'Doing covers is great, even if I come under pressure for doing them. I think they have more than earned their place on the album and they carry a bit of *Pop Idol* history with them, which is great. Everyone likes a bit of nostalgia!'

At this stage the album was still very much a work-in-progress, and Will was feeling incredibly grateful that he had been given the opportunity to take his time with it. 'I think you should always be conscious of the fact that any job can be short-lived and you should always take steps to make it as long-lived as you can. That's why we haven't released an album straightaway. We've taken care to write songs I'm happy with. When we get the right songs, then we'll release the album. It's all about setting up a long-term future.'

One person who was in no doubt that Will had a glittering future ahead of him was Simon Cowell. Despite their past grievances, it appeared that he was fast becoming one of Will's biggest fans. 'Will is so unique that he will definitely have longevity. I think he will move from the pop world to singing soul. It's all about having the right songwriters for Will,' he remarked.

However, there were still problems bubbling underneath the surface with regard to Will and Gareth. Although they themselves got on brilliantly, people around them were again trying to stir up trouble by saying that Gareth was getting preferential treatment from their shared record company, BMG.

The *Sun* newspaper started a full-scale campaign to get to the bottom of things, and they emailed Simon Cowell a series of burning questions that the nation needed to know the answers to. Simon, with long-suffering patience (the 'Will versus Gareth' issue had been rumbling on for some months now), took time to respond to the paper's demands.

They asked: 'Why was Gareth's debut single released just three weeks after Will's?'

Simon replied: 'The vast majority of Will's singles had sold within the first two weeks and we also had 4.5 million people who voted for Gareth. They were desperate for Gareth's record to come out. We tried to keep both sets of fans happy.'

The *Sun* also enquired: 'Why did Gareth include the same songs as Will's first single on his own debut?'

Simon hit back: 'Because the vote on *Pop Idol* was so close and we had recorded both songs with both of them. We had a huge amount of Gareth fans who wanted Gareth's versions of "Evergreen" and "Anything Is Possible".'

Meanwhile, BMG also put out a statement saying: 'We are totally committed to Will Young and have been from the minute he became the nation's Pop Idol. Will's career will continue to develop over the next few months with the total backing of BMG.'

Will himself had no issues whatsoever with the way he was being treated. 'The fans were a bit cross that I was being unfairly treated, but that's sort of what happens in the industry. If it wasn't him, it was going to be someone else. And I was really happy to give way to him. I tried to break his legs but the security people wouldn't let me through!' he joked. 'We are very different artists. We are going in different directions, and it's all fine.

'The whole *Sun* campaign thing was quite flattering. I felt really bad about all that. People are looking at me, thinking it's something I've done, but it isn't me at all. I'm really so chuffed that the fans do kind of feel they should stick up for me, because that's absolutely lovely, but I'm treated fairly,' he said. 'People still want to play us off against each other. We are good friends and we get on well professionally and outside work.'

Even *Pop Idol* host Declan Donnelly had an opinion on the situation, saying: 'It's been tough on Will. He has not got everything he deserved and they have been unfair on him. I shouldn't really be saying this as I worked on the show, but I think it has not been great for him. He was the *Pop Idol* winner and they should have held back Gareth's single for a bit. But instead Gareth is getting all the glory.'

But Will forgot his troubles and got happy when he performed at the massive Party in the Park concert in early July, appearing alongside such acclaimed acts as Westlife, Ashanti and Bryan Adams. Will and fellow performer Gareth made an effort to show that they still got on as well as ever, and even shared a backstage dressing room.

Will performed 'Ain't No Sunshine', 'Evergreen' and 'Light My Fire', and as soon as he came off stage he headed for the media run where he did a series of TV, radio and magazine interviews. One interviewer confided that Will's was one of the best performances of the day; it had no doubt won him a huge number of new fans.

Will also came to the rescue of three damsels in distress that day. Atomic Kitten arrived late to the show, having been stuck in traffic, but when they rushed to the stage for their performance they were halted by a burly security guard, who failed to recognize the trio. But Will stepped in to put the steward right. 'This is Atomic Kitten. They're probably bigger pop stars than me and they're supposed to be on [stage] now. I think you'd better let them through,' Will told him in no uncertain terms. The girls were duly allowed to pass and were able to get on with their performance.

The Kitten's Natasha Hamilton later praised Will's gallant efforts and said: 'We were rushing around a bit and made a quick dash from our changing room to the stage. It was only when we tried to bound on that we were stopped in our tracks. They didn't have a clue who we were. I think they thought we were over-zealous fans trying to storm the stage. Luckily Will saved the day.'

And it wasn't just his pop compatriots that Will was making an impression on. He revealed that he'd had some incredible letters from his fans, which had made him realize just what a difference music can make to people's lives. 'It's difficult to make sense of the job sometimes, and I have letters from people [that help me to do that],' he said. 'I had letters from a few people actually who were depressed during *Pop Idol*, and you know, they've said that watching the show and seeing me perform, and others, got them out of their depression and they're doing really well now. There was one lady who I think was about sixty-three. I can't remember where she came from, but she said, "I wasn't really listening to music and I'd been depressed for ages." She hadn't listened to music since her husband had died, because her love of music had gone. And then she said, "Recently I've bought a new stereo. I'm listening to music again." And I just think that things like that are just what it's all about really, you know? Things like that really touch, and make you realize just why you're doing the job you do.'

As the summer continued, Will and Gareth proved once and for all that there were no problems between them when they duetted on the Beatles' classic track 'The Long And Winding Road', which was eventually released as a single in September 2002, garnering Will another number one hit. The song had gone down brilliantly when the pair had performed it together on *Pop Idol*, and releasing it gave them a chance to show people that they really did get along.

'It is a real honour to cover a Beatles track,' said Will. 'I have always been a fan of theirs. After the brilliant response we got to it on the show, and as a thank you to our fans, we felt it would be a great track to celebrate a great year.'

Will and Gareth enjoyed the opportunity to spend time in each other's company again, and to put the niggling rumours of rivalry to rest for the final time. When he was asked what it was like spending so much time with Gareth, Will laughed, 'He's unbearable! I've said this time and time again but people think I'm joking. The man is unbearable!'

It's surprising, in light of former events, that his throwaway comment didn't spark another media frenzy. But for once the press remained silent on the subject. Perhaps, at last, they had grown tired of writing up the non-existent 'rivalry' of two such clearly good friends.

Will and Gareth had also planned to record a duet for the B-side of the single, a cover of Elvis's 'Suspicious Minds'. But Will decided that it wasn't for him and instead Gareth recorded the track on his own. 'Although I was invited to join Gareth to duet on "Suspicious Minds", I was uncomfortable with the track and suggested he did it solo as it suits his voice well,' Will explained. 'It sounds fantastic and I hope both tracks go down equally well.'

Will's version of Jackie Wilson's 'I Get The Sweetest Feeling' was also included as a bonus track.

Even though Will had loved working with Gareth again, he was quick to declare that it wasn't the start of a long series of duets, and there would be no 'Will and Gareth' album released off the back of the single. *Pop Idol* had been, after all, a search for a solo singing sensation, and both performers were keen to assert their own musical identities. However, there was to be a joint tour for the two pop stars. But it was to mark the end of an era rather than to signify that the duo would be teaming up consistently in the future. 'It's been so much fun doing the duet. Doing a song with someone else and getting to know Gareth better has been great,' said Will. 'We're just getting to know each other better out of the context of the competition. Before, even though we never had a problem with it, we were against each other in the competition. I think that after the tour we will go our separate ways. It will be a friendly farewell! Both Gareth and I will move on and take the different musical routes we both wish to follow.'

Nevertheless, Will added: 'But it's not like going separate ways and never speaking to each other again. The single is kind of like tying it all up and saying a fond farewell to the show, then we will do the tour together, then my album comes out and his will come out later, and that's it. I think it's been the right kind of time frame and we'll go on and try and make successes of our careers. Hopefully long may they last.'

The duo recorded the video for their duet in Blackheath, south-east London, in early August 2002, and were thrilled with the result. It was directed by Tim Royles, while Bailey Walsh, who directed Will's 'Light My Fire' video, was the executive producer.

Tim Royles wrote a 'treatment', a short description of his aims for the film, which claimed the video would be: 'A timeless performance, without gimmick or artifice, a showcase to demonstrate Will and Gareth's extraordinary vocal abilities. Skilfully crafted simplicity is the key to this one-take performance video. The strength and classic nature of this video reminds us of Simon and Garfunkel as they performed their free concert in New York's Central Park. The look of the video is reminiscent of Blue Note Jazz record covers.'

When it was screened in all its glory, the promo was proclaimed a winner. It was slick, mature and simple, with the lads looking like true stars. But although to everyone watching it appeared that it was all filmed in one very long, very impressive take – the 'one-take performance video' of Royles's passionate treatment – Will revealed otherwise: 'We had to warm up, obviously, to get us into it. I think we did about fifteen takes because I kept on making mistakes. Gareth was absolutely perfect, but I kept on making mistakes at the beginning.'

With the duet done and dusted, Will was finally able to put the finishing touches to his solo album on Friday 8 August. 'It felt absolutely amazing,' he said happily. 'It was one of those moments where I stood back and thought, "I must enjoy this moment," and I had a real kind of smile on my face. I sent a message to my friend going, "Oh, I can't believe I'm doing this, this is amazing." And I had a celebratory drink. I was really happy.

'I chose all the songs, put them in an order and that was pretty cool. It's good to sit back and think, "Actually, this is really cool. I did that and I'm really glad I did."'

And Will reiterated once again how pleased he was that the album hadn't been rush-released after the TV show had finished, and how that extra time had truly benefited the album he'd produced. 'Since *Pop Idol*, I have wanted to spend as much time as possible writing and co-writing with some great singers and songwriters in the studio, rather than recording new tracks for immediate release,' he commented. 'Hopefully it will mean that my first album will be as good as it possibly can be, and will get a great response.'

But Will had a while to wait for that feedback. The record wasn't scheduled for release until October, so for the time being both critics and fans were in the dark about the contents of the much-anticipated collection. As Will's record company geared up for the big release, the singer himself had an important trip to the States to prepare for. In September Will got his first bit of exposure on a grand scale in America, when he was invited to perform on the final of *American Idol*, the US equivalent of *Pop Idol*, which boasted a weekly audience of over 20 million viewers. As there were plans to launch Will in America at some point in the future, this was a massive step in the right direction in getting him recognized globally.

But despite Will being aware of the massive viewing figures – and having himself experienced first-hand the huge national popularity of *Pop Idol* in the UK – it wasn't until he landed in America that he realized just how big a deal the programme was. 'I kind of missed all of the build-up to the US show, so I wasn't really sure what I was letting myself in for. At customs the guy was like, "What are you here for?" And I went, "I'm singing on the *American Idol* final." His reaction made me realize that it was a pretty big show.'

Will chose to perform 'I Get The Sweetest Feeling' for his American debut, as well as a duet of Diana Ross's 'Ain't No Mountain High Enough', with the show's eventual winner, Kelly Clarkson, and he received a rapturous reception from the studio audience. But he wasn't quite as confident as he seemed. 'On *Pop Idol* I had the backing of the show. Here I'm unknown,' he said nervously.

And he certainly felt anonymous when he was drafted into the after-show press conference – where none of the US journalists had a clue who he was. Not one of them bothered to ask him a question, so he decided to have some fun and randomly picked a journalist out and said: 'Yes, can I have your question, please?' Needless to say, the room remained silent, and Will admits that he doesn't think they really understood his humour.

'In America, they seemed rather amused by the idea that I was the first Pop Idol. They thought I needed to show more attitude. I felt very English!' he confessed.

Even the American public weren't particularly polite to him. One lady came up to him and said: 'Oh, you have great teeth. Oh no, the top ones are awful.' Thankfully Will saw the funny side. 'She was so rude it was brilliant,' he recalls. It's an American stereotype that the British have bad teeth. Even back in London the Yanks continued to harp on about his dental work; while Will was eating in a restaurant one night, an American woman approached him. She didn't ask for an autograph though – instead she told him that he'd never make it in the States without improving his gnashers! Will's response? 'I bit her. Not really, but I thought about it!'

After returning to the UK, despite some pressure from his record company to release songs in the US and Asian markets, Will decided that he was keen to keep his attentions on Europe for the time being. 'I wanted to concentrate on the writing craft. Last year was the whole fame and promotional experience, it was all a bit crazy, and I felt it was time for me to try and mature as an artist. I wouldn't have been able to have done that if I was going, "Hi, I'm everywhere,"' he said.

As it was, Will's writing craft was about to be put to the test. On 7 October 2002, after six months in the making, Will's debut album, *From Now On*, was released. Having heard so much about it from Will over the past few months, his fans finally had the chance to make up their own minds about the collection.

Will was overjoyed that his album was finally out in the public domain, but the singer was also undoubtedly worried about whether or not it would be a hit. He even sent a friend out to record shops in the first week of release, to see how the record was selling – but he needn't have worried. It sold over 56,000 copies on its first day, and by the end of the week 187,000 copies had been shifted, meaning that it went straight to number one.

A review on the BBC website raved, 'Will finally gets to prove himself with tunes of his own backed by orchestras and choirs. Of these, standing out on first listen is "Lovestruck", featuring quirky rhythmic vocals but nevertheless meeting all pop criteria. It's a fab album that won't disappoint anyone. It'll be a sure-fire Christmas stocking filler for everyone from pop chicks to their Robson-and-Jerome-loving grans.'

Still buzzing from this latest triumph, Will announced that his next single, the double A-sided 'You And I'/'Don't Let Me Down', was to be the official song of 2002's Children In Need. The charity's annual day of televised fund-raising was scheduled to take place on 15 November, and Will was already looking forward to helping out.

The tracks would be Will's first original song releases, and he reckoned that the timing was perfect. 'I want to release my very first original track at a very special time. I have chosen to do this for Children In Need as I know there is a huge demand for the single, so hopefully I will be able to raise as much money as possible for such a good cause.'

But that excitement was still to come. October had yet another treat in store for Will, and saw the star's induction into the fashion hall of fame, when he graced the pages of style bible *Vogue* magazine.

The feature was a tribute to TV shows, and Will appeared alongside his old friend Gareth. Will was stunned that they'd been asked to appear in one of the most prestigious fashion magazines in the world. 'Us? In *Vogue*? When they called, I was sure they'd made a mistake,' he says.

The pair were shot in London's Park Studios by well-respected photographer Nick Knight. 'We had this really famous photographer who I've never heard of, which was quite embarrassing. But I sort of pretended I had. He's called Nick Knight, and I thought they said Michael Knight, so I said, "Wasn't he the guy from *Knight Rider*?" No one laughed, so I decided to keep quiet,' said a red-faced Will.

Despite his obliviousness when it came to the photographer, the results of the shoot were incredible, with Will looking super-toned in dark trousers and a damp white shirt, which was pulled open to reveal his torso. Will claimed in the accompanying *Vogue* article: 'Gareth is better-looking than me.' But looking at the finished pictures, there are many who would disagree.

When Will was asked afterwards whether he would be branching out into modelling, he replied: 'I don't think so! I looked a bit of a plonker, so I don't think I'll do it again. But it would be quite nice. It depends. I mean, if they were really nice clothes I think I might do it. But you know what [I'm like], I might trip up again or something stupid; everyone would laugh at me.'

Two weeks later Will won his first ever industry awards, when he walked away with the accolades for Favourite UK Male Singer and Favourite Newcomer at the inaugural National Music Awards, where he also performed 'You And I'.

But Gareth didn't go home empty-handed either, picking up the award for Favourite TV Performance. A thrilled Will said afterwards, 'I'm really happy, I can't put it into words. I haven't actually got the awards; they took them away. I'm very lucky to be doing the job I want. I'm quite happy to get up and work. This job is everything I wanted it to be.'

The beauty of it was, with his debut album now under his belt, Will's glittering career was only just beginning.

CHAPTER NINE

A Dream Comes True

Will had had such a fantastic time on the *Pop Idol* tour that he was keen to hit the road again as soon as possible. This time he teamed up with *Pop Idol* chums Gareth and Zoe Birkett, on an extensive tour around Britain that was called simply 'Will and Gareth'. Zoe was thrilled to be asked along as the special guest and said, 'I'm looking forward to touring with two of the best-looking guys in the UK.' And who wouldn't be?

The tour kicked off in London's Docklands Arena on 3 October 2002, only a day after Will filmed the video for his upcoming single, 'You And I'. The late running of the video shoot meant that Will was tired before the tour had even begun – but that didn't stop him being eager to be back in front of big crowds again.

Will said: 'We've only just finished the full *Pop Idol* tour, which was great. But this will be just the three of us, so it will be extra special. Zoe was brought in for the tour because she received such a great reception last time. By the end of this tour, we will have performed to over 500,000 fans. Our fans are the people who gave us this opportunity, so it means the world to us. To be getting back on the road and performing live for the second time in one year is fantastic, and to be going with Gareth and Zoe is the icing on the cake.'

The tour also stopped off in Birmingham, Nottingham, Manchester, Sheffield, Newcastle and Glasgow, and rounded off in Minehead on 2 November, where the trio got a lovely surprise. 'I have an official website that sent me flowers and champagne at every single place I went to,' Will revealed. 'And on the last night, which was at Butlins in Minehead, they sent champagne and flowers to Zoe and Gareth as well. I thought that was a really nice touch coming from my fans, you know. My fan base are just lovely people and they're so supportive and it just makes it worthwhile.'

Will found that he soon got used to being on the road again and actually started to enjoy the travelling lifestyle. 'I like the regularity of it,' he said. 'You wake up and go to a new place, you do the gig and so on. It's very self-contained.'

Of all his hits, Will enjoyed performing 'You And I' the most on tour, but it wasn't all fun. He had an on-stage disaster one night, when he lost his footing walking down a set of stairs while doing a duet with Zoe. He tried to carry on regardless, by lounging sexily on the steps and pretending it was part of the show – he just about got away with it, but still blushes when he recalls the incident.

The fans who were stuck at the backs of the arenas were not forgotten, and Will and Gareth made sure they were in for a treat during the tour. The singers had arranged to have a 'B' stage built, which they walked along when they duetted, which meant that all the people in the so-called 'cheap seats' had a great view of their idols, as opposed to them appearing as a couple of tiny dots on a very big stage very far away. Will and Gareth both felt it was important that everyone who went to the shows got to see their idols. 'We wanted it to be fair and for everyone to get to see us, and because of the "B" stage even the people right at the back got to see us up close. It's not fair for them to come along to a show and not be able to see us very well, so the "B" stage made a real difference,' explained Gareth.

Once again, the press raved about Will's performances at the gigs. Music website Dotmusic commented: 'Will's voice is the winner. See, real life is just like the telly after all.' The *Telegraph*, meanwhile, was convinced that Will had even more up his sleeve and would no doubt reveal more at future shows: 'Ending his solo set, he congratulated us on our taste after cheekily mishearing the crowd's hysterical requests for "Light My Fire" as "Oh! 'Signed, Sealed And Delivered' by Stevie Wonder? Super!" The vocal acrobatics he displayed on *Pop Idol*, however, were hidden away for safe-keeping, presumably for the day he finally rests himself from the all-singing variety triple-bill. He's the one to watch.'

And watching Will perform was something the fans at the shows couldn't help but do. From the moment he arrived on stage, singing the eerie, atmospheric melody of 'Ain't No Sunshine', Will commanded entire arenas with his voice and presence. His set, which was scheduled third behind Zoe's warm-up act and Gareth's pop-tastic performance, was truly a case of saving the best till last. As he warbled his way through a varied set list, which included favourites ('Evergreen'), new songs ('You And I'), and a handful of covers ('I Get The Sweetest Feeling'), Will created a chilled-out, effortless vibe which made for a joyful night. And he was joined on stage by both Zoe and Gareth for duets with each, before the trio brought the house down with a three-way rendition of the Al Green smash, 'Let's Stay Together'.

In short, a good time was had by all, and needless to say Zoe Birkett treasured her time with the boys. 'I love working with these guys,' she said. 'We are such good friends and it's great being on stage with them. I enjoy being the only girl. I get treated like royalty and have a dressing room to myself.'

But anyone hoping the three idols would team up for a single release was going to be disappointed. 'It would be great to release a song as a trio, but the problem is we'd all be fighting for the microphone!' joked Will.

Come November, Will opened Children In Need 2002 with a rendition of 'I Get The Sweetest Feeling'. As part of the money-raising drive, viewers had the opportunity to pay money to call in and win a performance from Will in their living room that very night. The competition was won by a lucky girl from Exeter, and Will was swiftly transported down there in a private jet, treating her, her friends and her neighbours to an exclusive mini-gig.

Will was left very moved by the evening and revealed that he had done his best to become involved in the charity in the run-up to the big night, so that he could gain more understanding of what it was all about.

'I do think it's important to look up the things that you're supporting and going into,' he said. 'So I went to see a shelter for women and children who'd suffered domestic violence, and obviously I can't say where it was, but it was very interesting for me, because I'd actually done a dissertation on domestic violence ... It was a wonderful day. It was about these women who'd become empowered and left these relationships and had become stronger and were so much happier for it. It was a real eye-opener.'

Domestic violence is an issue about which Will feels passionately – and he is also conscious of the fact that public perception of the problem is not always wholly accurate, which concerns him. His dissertation investigated the middle-class phenomenon of domestic violence and how it is frequently ignored or covered up – an approach that has since been further explored by the charity Refuge, with its national awareness-raising campaign. Though Will acknowledges that he himself couldn't begin to say what needs to change to improve the current situation, he concludes simply yet powerfully: 'I hate bullying wherever I find it.'

Will has always had strong views on domestic violence, hence him writing his university dissertation on the subject. His research also led him to write a screenplay about the issue, which he hopes to develop when he gets the time. 'It's a very English film about domestic violence. I'm working on it with a friend. I don't know if I'd be good enough to act in it,' he said.

November was quite a month for Will, and as the festive season loomed ever closer he was invited to switch on the Regent Street Christmas lights. In the run-up to the big event he said, 'To be switching on the lights in the capital is going to be a really special end to a fantastic year. As soon as the lights go on, you feel very Christmassy and really start to get into the spirit of things. I hope that lots of people come along and give me a chance to thank them for their support by singing live at this free event. I'm really looking forward to it!'

And he wasn't disappointed. Thousands of elated Christmas shoppers and fans turned up to hear him perform the Children In Need singles, 'You And I' and 'Don't Let Me Down'. They were also treated to Will's gorgeous rendition of 'Walking In A Winter Wonderland', which put everybody in the Christmas spirit.

Will's life now included private jets, a number one album and the coveted showbiz job of turning on the Christmas lights. So was he feeling like a superstar yet? 'I'm quite proud of the way I've handled it all. I really don't feel famous,' he revealed. 'You can become paranoid about it, and some people actually start to look for it, you know, to check that people are looking at them. But I went out in Hampstead last night and not one person recognized me. People don't recognize you as much as you'd think.'

Will doesn't exactly court the crazy celeb lifestyle though. Forget hanging out at the Met Bar or spending thousands of pounds shopping on Bond Street, all Will really wants is some peace and quiet in his life. When asked what his ideal weekend would entail, he replied, 'I'd get on a sleeper train at King's Cross on Friday night and wake up in Inverness on Saturday morning. I'd spend the weekend going for walks and sitting in pubs.' Not your traditional rock 'n' roll response – but then, that's Will all over.

'You And I'/'Don't Let Me Down' was released on 25 November and charted at number two. It was kept off the top spot by Christina Aguilera's raunchy single 'Dirrty', but despite Will's record not getting to number one, he was still pleased with his high entry and happy that the single had raised a hefty amount for Children In Need. 'I think the single was a step on – the video, the song and the styling, the whole way we did it. I also think the fact that it went to number two was a good thing,' Will reflected. 'If you keep getting number ones all the time you are going to go downhill at some point, but I needed that to happen to take the pressure off.'

That December, Will was asked to perform at a carol concert at St Luke's Church in London, in aid of the Nordoff-Robbins charity. It was a huge honour for him to be asked to carry out the role, which had previously been filled by such esteemed performers as Annie Lennox and Robbie Williams.

On arrival at the venue, Will spotted a swarm of photographers who were poised outside, all desperate to get pictures of him. To try to lessen the attention on himself, Will left it until the last possible moment to walk into the church. What he didn't realize, however, was that the 1,000 or so people who were attending the concert had already taken their seats, so that when he walked in he had to make his way to his seat – which was right up at the front of the church – in full view of everyone. To make matters worse, he was wearing very noisy shoes that day, so he made quite an entrance. It was the sort of 'diva' moment that always makes Will cringe; he was mightily embarrassed. As he meekly took his place next to some friends who were also attending the concert, they wasted no time in mercilessly teasing him about his dramatic arrival at the church.

Shortly before Christmas, Will was invited to perform at the Royal Variety Show, and also to introduce some of the other acts performing, which ranged from ventriloquists to singers such as Shania Twain and Anastacia.

The evening was all the more enjoyable for Will as his brother Rupert was working at the show as a runner, specifically looking after Kylie Minogue, so they got to spend some time together. Fun as the event was, though, Will is still slightly embarrassed about the night, for when he was introducing people he decided to veer from the script he had been given and instead try out a few of his own jokes. His plan went awry, however, when no one laughed along with him – and he even suspects that when the concert was later shown on TV, some canned laughter had been added in, to make him appear funnier than he actually was live.

Still, it wasn't a totally disastrous evening. Will was thrilled to get the chance to meet one of his all-time heroes, the late comedian Bob Monkhouse, who was also at the show. 'Bob turned to me and said, "I think you are a very funny man. I saw you on Graham Norton's show and I thought you were great," and I said, "Well, coming from you that's a real compliment." He seemed very wise and I was really touched by him. I wrote him a letter after the event, saying how pleased I was to meet him and checking that he was okay. I hope he got it.'

December continued to fly by in a whirl of prestigious performances and gigs, and before 2002 was out Will realized one of his greatest ambitions, when he appeared in *The Play What I Wrote* at London's Wyndham's Theatre. The show was a critically acclaimed play based around a tribute to the legendary Morecambe and Wise, and was directed by highbrow thespian Kenneth Branagh. Every night, a different celebrity would guest-star in the play, and the likes of Jude Law and Roger Moore had already taken their turns.

Will, having already seen the play, had always secretly hoped that he would be asked to participate at some stage. And when the long-awaited call came through inviting him to take part, he dedicated many hours to learning the script and attending rehearsals.

At last, the time came for him to don the various costumes – which included a huge white wig, a smoking jacket and a pink ball gown – and make his West End debut. Will did himself proud. He played the role for two nights and when it was time to pass the mantle over to the next guest – the highly acclaimed actress Miranda Richardson, of whom Will is a big fan – he had to write a message to her on the wall of the dressing room. His message read: 'Dear Countess Toblerone. Please ignore what you have read in the papers. I am indeed your straight husband and I love you lots. (Actually I do. I really love you.)'

Will had always relished theatre, being heavily involved in drama while he was at university, but his West End experience now gave him even more of a taste for acting, and he yearned to perform in a musical, when the time was right. Will certainly didn't see the genre as a career swansong, as some performers do. With his Arts Ed background and *Oklahoma!* experience, he appreciated the complexity of staging and singing such shows, and knew a musical would be an exciting challenge to take on, in good time.

All in all, Will crammed more into one year in 2002 than most people manage in ten. His exceptional achievements included landing a record deal (after winning the biggest talent show the country had ever seen), releasing singles (most of which reached number one), setting British records, performing to hundreds of thousands of people on tours around the country, performing for royalty, and appearing in a West End show. It had been one hell of a ride.

Will ended the year on a high, reflecting on an incredible twelve months which saw him transform from an aspiring singer to one of the most highly regarded performers in Britain.

Said the ever down-to-earth star: 'I came into this to sing, not for the fame, and I have to say I don't care for the fame that much. And I'm glad I don't, because otherwise my head would be so big it would be in the clouds. I just see the fame as a necessary means to an end. Quite simply, this is what I was always meant to do. This is the job that suits me. I have a hundred per cent job satisfaction.'

With enthusiasm like that, 2003 looked set to be bigger, better and even more mind-blowing than 2002.

CHAPTER TEN

A Great BRIT

Will waved goodbye to the madness of 2002 by spending New Year's Eve in Cornwall with close friends, and then took a well-deserved holiday on the instructions of his management company, 19.

He headed off to Paris for a few days to shop and chill out, but work was soon on his mind again and, in particular, his next album. Even though he was ordered to go away and totally relax, he found himself sending emails to people at work at two o'clock in the morning, filled with ideas of people he could work with, TV shows he could appear on and things he could do in order to promote his second album.

Exactly the same thing happened when he headed to Mexico later in January with his friends Claire and Hugh, for two weeks of beach-based relaxation. He took a Dictaphone with him to record his thoughts and ideas for new songs, and would even use it while he was lying around in the sun, supposedly clearing his head.

When his Dictaphone broke (probably from over-use), Will called his mobile from his very expensive hotel phone instead, singing ideas to its voicemail facility to ensure that he would have a permanent record of his inspirations. However, he confesses that when he actually listened to the phone messages, they didn't always sound *quite* as good as he'd imagined they would, so maybe the calls weren't quite as necessary as he'd first thought. At the time, though, Will didn't want to forget anything, and thought it better to be safe than sorry.

Despite all this work, however, Will still managed to unwind a little bit. As is his preference, as well as spending some nights staying in the kinds of places in which you would expect to find a top pop star, he also kept it real by choosing a few 'studenty' places for accommodation, as a way of getting himself in touch with the real world again.

'When I go away I make a point of backpacking and staying in youth hostels,' he says. 'Of course it's nice to stay a couple of days in a bit of luxury, but [the youth hostels] make you realize you're not very important because back home you get trumped up about yourself.'

Will was brought back down to earth with a bump on holiday, when he discovered that being a leading pop star doesn't guarantee you a good spot at karaoke. When he and his friends went out to a bar to celebrate his birthday, Will, buoyed by a few drinks, got up and sang 'Light My Fire' on karaoke. But his fellow revellers decided he wasn't good enough to sing lead, and he was given backing vocals to do instead.

Yet the conspicuous Will tones soon got a group of British air hostesses in a flap, when they recognized his voice and came running in from a bar next door. Even in the middle of Mexico, Will found himself being recognized. Does he ever get sick of the constant attention? 'It's just part of the job, really,' he says. 'It's lovely when people say nice things, and it's not so nice when people say nasty things. Sometimes you're in your own little world and you're pottering around and it can be quite daunting, and other times it's really nice. I've kind of got used to it, but you have to remind yourself that it's slightly surreal that people know your name. When you're walking through Covent Garden and people are saying, "Hi, Will!" it can be strange.'

In January Will came second in *Heat* magazine's 'Fifty Sexiest Celebrities in Showbiz' poll – as would have been Will's own first choice, the delicious David Beckham topped the vote. *Heat* cooed: 'Will Young – he's got a smile that would light up the Royal Albert Hall, and impeccable manners. Okay, so we ladies know we're never going to strike lucky with the *Pop Idol* winner, but we don't care. With his natty dress sense, incredible voice and oodles of charm, Will is a true star.'

No sooner had Will arrived home from Mexico than he was jetting off again, this time to Italy to promote 'Light My Fire', which went straight to number two in the Italian charts. He was going down a storm in the fashionable country, where he had become a style icon, having done shoots for über-cool magazines *L'Uomo Vogue* and *Café Latte*. 'I knew it would go well in Italy. I love the country, anyway, the people and the lifestyle,' Will said. The coolness of the Italian people meant that he rarely got bothered in public, too – something which he enjoyed immensely.

Germany followed, and despite some initial reservations about having to go away again, due to tiredness and missing his home comforts, the trip went well and Will has since become one of the country's most popular stars.

Jet-set lifestyle and international acclaim aside, however, back home in Britain Will was still garnering as much respect as ever – and by now it wasn't just his legion of fans who were singing his praises: the music industry bigwigs were jumping on the bandwagon too. In February 2003 Will was recognized on a big scale in the record business when he was awarded his very first industry honour at the highly prestigious BRIT awards. As accolades go, this was one of the very best.

It would have been impossible for anyone not to see that he had already made a huge mark on the tough music market since winning *Pop Idol* – in terms of sales and press coverage alone he was practically a one-man phenomenon – but sceptics were still questioning whether he had true staying power. Once the buzz from the TV show wore off, would he still be a star?

The year before, Robbie Williams had shown great foresight (probably unintentionally) when he picked up his award for Best British Male Solo Artist in 2002, just days before Will released his debut single. Turning to the celebrity-packed audience Robbie made a joke about Will trying to steal his pop crown, saying, 'I'm too strong, buddy, I'm too big for you. You want to come and take the food for my kids off my table, but this is my third BRIT. Craig David couldn't do it, so what makes you think you can?' If only he'd known.

When he heard about the homage, Will laughed: 'Apparently Robbie Williams had a jokey dig at me in his BRIT awards acceptance speech last night and it's all over the papers today. Wow – I'm flattered! I can't believe Robbie would even know who the hell I was!'

But just a year later, Will followed in Robbie's designer footsteps when he went along to the BRITs at London's Earl's Court Arena with a whopping *three* nominations, for Best British Breakthrough Act, Best British Single (for 'Evergreen'/'Anything Is Possible') and Best Pop Act – with the latter two categories also featuring nominations for his close friend Gareth Gates.

When Will first heard he had been nominated, he headed to the nearest record shop and bought albums by all the artists in the breakthrough category, so that he could see what he was up against. He soon became convinced that Miss Dynamite would be victorious.

He was so nervous in the run-up to the big night that he even contemplated pretending he was ill so he didn't have to attend. 'I was beating myself up a bit about having three nominations. I was putting myself down and I don't think I was giving myself any credit at all,' he confesses. 'I was almost joining all the anti-*Idol* people. Being nominated for a BRIT was something I had always dreamed of and when it happened, I felt as if other people may not think I deserved it and I was in a bit of a fluster about it.'

As ever, the BRITs bash was a glitzy affair packed to the rafters with celebrities, press and record-company execs, all eager to find out who the lucky winners would be.

Once again Will's nerves got the better of him on the journey to Earl's Court. 'I'd got a bottle of Rescue Remedy at the ready and, despite the fact that you are only supposed to have a few drops, I downed it like a shot of tequila,' he reveals.

Nerves steadied, on his arrival at the ceremony Will discovered that he had been seated down the front, in full view of the crowd. He was ecstatic to see a collection of banners bearing his name. 'That made me feel less nervous and gave me a real lift,' he explains.

Once seated, Will had only to endure the agony of waiting for his categories to be announced. It felt like the moment would never come, but then all too soon DJ Sara Cox was striding up to the microphone and listing the nominations for the Best British Breakthrough Act. For Will, this category was the biggie, the award that he had most coveted – and also been most anxious about. And the winner is ...?

After what felt like forever to Will, Sara announced that the *Pop Idol* winner had been chosen by the listeners of Radio 1 as the most deserving recipient of the Best British Breakthrough Act award. Instantly, the crowd went wild, screaming and shouting out his name. Competition may have been tough – Liberty X, The Coral, The Streets and, of course, Ms Dynamite were also nominated in the category – but Will had triumphed over them all.

In an industry that builds you up to knock you down, no one is more at risk of backbiting and bitter critics than reality-TV-show stars, who are often mocked no matter how talented they are. But when Will scooped his first BRIT, it silenced the cynics and sent out a message to everyone that he had true talent, and that he was here to stay.

Despite his shock Will still managed to give a moving speech, saying: 'I don't know what to say; I was too busy clapping for Ms Dynamite. I'd like to first of all thank Simon Fuller, my manager, who's a wonderful guy. It really makes a difference to have a manager who I see eye to eye with and who tells me when I have really bad ideas, which is quite often. I'd also like to thank 19 and BMG. I have a really wonderful team of people who I work with and I wouldn't be here if it wasn't for them. I'd also like to dedicate the award to two of my friends who aren't very well at the moment, James and Sarah, and I hope you get better soon. And I've got one more thing to say – thank you very much to you guys for voting. You're always voting! I'll see you next year. Cheers.'

Yet despite sounding very eloquent, Will swears that he didn't have a thank-you speech planned. 'I honestly didn't, and I think you could tell! But there were two things I knew I wanted to do. I had two friends who were unfortunately very ill. One friend was going through chemotherapy and another was going through keyhole surgery in the same week, and [all] I remembered was that I wanted to dedicate the award to them. That put things in perspective.'

After the show Will admitted that winning took him totally by surprise. 'I wasn't expecting it. And if there was an award I wanted to win, it was that one because it was a great accolade. It felt amazing. I think that's why I felt that after winning it, I needed to live up to the title. I was really pleased. There are not many times when I'm really lost for words and speechless and let myself go and enjoy the moment, but that was definitely one of them.'

Once the show had ended, Will made sure he celebrated in true pop-star style by supping champagne – and lots of it. His first bottle was handed to him backstage by his old friend Dr Fox, during an interview for Capital FM.

Clutching his award, Will told Foxy, '[Winning the award] is definitely my best moment ... ever. It doesn't take it away from any of the things that happened last year or have happened this year, but I do think that particular category means so much. The other people that were in that category are incredible artists and I was really chuffed for me just to be nominated. I was very surprised to win.'

Award in hand, Will then headed off to the BRITs official party, which was held in a huge room next to the ceremony. 'As I walked in there were two lines, 50 metres long, of people holding drinks. I said, "Let's go for it!" I would have been happy just going from tray to tray! It turned out to be a very drunken affair. I was on a real high and remember trying to phone all my friends, screaming down the phone with excitement.'

However, the night didn't end there. Will did a sneaky re-route back home to his flat, which was just around the corner from Earl's Court, to freshen up, before heading on to another do which was being held by his record company, BMG, at hip members' club Home House. Here he hooked up with people from his management company, as well as with friends and colleagues from BMG, and had a great time toasting his success with the various teams, sitting on the floor and swigging from his glass. The revelry continued till the wee small hours – it was 5 a.m. before a very tired, very happy, and very drunk Mr Young retired to bed.

Will went to sleep cuddling his BRIT that night and didn't let go of it for the next twenty-five hours. He had found a new friend. Who cared if it was only ten inches tall and made of metal?

And where does he keep his award now? 'It's in my bedroom. It has pride of place, and I look at it very fondly when I'm sitting on the loo!'

Will acknowledges that winning the award spurred him on to start work on his next album as soon as possible, as it gave him a huge boost. 'I had about six weeks off at the beginning of 2003 and the first thing I did was the BRITs, and I actually think that getting the British Breakthrough award there gave me a kick up the backside. It gave me something to work for. I always think that at awards ceremonies no one is better than anyone else, but getting an award is almost like a responsibility in a way. I kind of thought I had better live up to that responsibility.'

Winning such a prestigious award also meant that there was even more pressure on Will, as expectations for his career rose. But he took it in his stride. 'It's not a bad thing that people expect more of me. That makes me push myself more, which can only be positive.'

Through all this acclaim and excitement, Will was still managing to stay true to himself. A manager at Will's publisher, Contender Books, who worked closely with Will on his book *By Public Demand* around this time, recalls how he didn't once play the diva, despite his growing success. 'I first met Will when we were doing photos for his book, about a year after he'd won *Pop Idol*,' she remembers. 'We went on a boat trip up the Thames to get some shots and he spent a lot of time texting his friends and chatting with people. He was with his PA, Faye, and he was really charming and friendly and willing to do whatever we asked of him. He was also very professional. He made me feel really welcome and even invited me to the pub with him and the rest of the crew.'

Will hinted at the fact that he had already made quite a lot of money off the back of *Pop Idol*, though he probably wasn't aware of how it all sounded. His new, rather impressive bank balance was simply a fact of life for the singer, and his conversations and life choices now necessarily took that bigger bank balance into account. 'He was talking about all these trendy bars he'd been to and about how he'd like to buy one of the flats at the side of the river, which cost a fortune,' the publisher said. 'It made me think about how far he'd come in a year if he could afford one of those!'

Not surprisingly, she recalls that Will was recognized everywhere he went, and was incredibly friendly to people and more than happy to sign autographs. 'He was nice to everyone. His PA kept trying to get him away because there was work to be done, but he kept saying, "Just one more!" When we got off the boat at Greenwich we bought ice creams, and Will stayed for ages chatting to the guy that was selling them. Everyone else was ready to move on, but he was happy to stand there talking away. All of a sudden people started to come out of shops and houses, as word got around that he was there. We had to dash off then, but he would have been quite happy to stay for ages longer. He didn't say no to one person who asked for his autograph.'

And Will displayed the same friendly manner when Contender Books held a party for the launch of the book, at swish Notting Hill bar Julie's. 'He turned up on time and worked the room really well. He had a minder-type person with him, but he stopped to chat with everyone and seemed to really enjoy himself. He also had a couple of mates with him, but they waited until he'd done his work before they all hung out together. He was so professional.'

Will was especially kind to one young fan who was a bit overcome at meeting such a big star. 'I took my daughter along with me,' the publisher confides. 'She was three at the time but she knew who he was because she'd watched *Pop Idol*. He was so sweet with her and posed for photos and kept waving at her across the room. He was outside with his friends when we left and he said a special goodbye to her and told her she was lovely. She was very taken with him!'

So does Will's former publisher think that his friendliness is genuine, or has he simply been very well trained? 'I think he's totally genuine,' she says. 'He's been really well brought up and is so polite. He must meet people like me every day but he remembered me the second time I met him, which definitely says something. He seems to have managed to have kept his feet firmly on the ground.'

Much of this positive attitude was down to the fact that Will understood being a pop star involves lots of hard work. You're only ever as good as your last record, and while *From Now On* had brought Will much credibility and success, he was keen to get cracking with the all-important follow-up. For Will, the second album was his first real chance to put his own original stamp on the music industry, in a fully creative sense, and he was determined that everything should be right.

So with the first album still selling bucketloads, Will began thinking long and hard about the second collection. He had already begun coming up with ideas on his holiday and had been furiously writing down lyrics whenever he got the chance.

At the beginning of 2003, he had reflected on what a crazy year 2002 had been, and took the decision that 2003 was going to be much more about the music than being seen in the public eye. Winning *Pop Idol* and riding the wave of that success had been phenomenal, but Will needed to come up with the goods to ensure his career would have longevity.

'I felt like I was starting from scratch, age twenty-four. I had the whole rise to success but it wasn't very well balanced and the musical side had to catch up,' he says of the hard work he had to do following the TV show. 'Maybe I was jumping through hoops, but I think it has been a necessary progression. Perhaps people don't think I had a part in creating the last album, but I co-wrote six songs. I don't know if I was saying everything I wanted to say, but it was hard work just trying to keep my head above water. This year, I really wanted to take time off to concentrate on the writing and the music.'

And that's exactly what he did. Once again he hooked up with Biff and Jules to work on some tracks, but also decided to try out some new styles. And that meant working with new writers and producers in order to get a feel for what he wanted. As well as Jonathan Shorten, who worked extensively with Gabrielle on her album *Rise*, Will went into the studio with Eg White, who has worked with Emiliana Torrini – one of Will's favourite artists. 'He's a bit of a genius. The music flows through him. I said to my manager, Simon Fuller, "If you can do anything, get me with this guy because he's cool." Simon goes, "Okay, I think you're mad, but anything to get you out of the country!"'

Will spent ten days in both Florida and LA, where he hooked up with a writer called Robin Thicke, a singer, writer and producer who has worked with the likes of Christina Aguilera, Marc Antony and Brian McKnight. The pair hit it off so well that Will reckons that they could have written an entire album 'within a month'. But he was keen to keep experimenting, and he also worked with Lester Mendez, Rick Nowels and Steve Morales – all hugely famous and much-respected songwriters. Will also collaborated with ex-Alisha's Attic singer Karen Poole, who has written for top acts such as the Sugababes and Kylie.

On this second album, Will was keen to put more of himself into the record: he wanted to delve deeper into his emotions with his songwriting, and step away from the kind of romantic, smoochy songs that had featured on his first album. 'Lyrics are what I was initially insecure about, and I remember people saying to me that on the last album they were a bit boring. I felt I had to believe in them this time around. I've tried to put a lot more of me into them, my experiences and the things that have gone on around me,' he said. 'I wanted to get away from relationship and love songs. I did that a lot on the last album, and I've never even been in a relationship! I have written about things going well and that is actually really personal to me. I've had shitty times like everyone else, and I'm having quite good times now, and it's cool to be able to articulate that.'

However, while he was in the US he encountered a rather awkward problem with one of the writers he worked with – although he won't say who. 'I remember writing with a songwriter in America who didn't know me and didn't know that I was gay. And his lyrics kept saying "girl" and they were quite personal. I was saying to him, "Hmmm, maybe we should do something else?" I didn't want to embarrass him because he was a lovely person. I didn't want to say, "Well, actually I'm gay," because he might have felt stupid. And I thought maybe if I just act a bit camper he may pick up on the fact!'

Yet it wasn't all work and no play for Will. Harking back to his days at Wellington and those old dreams of Olympic glory, Will still likes to keep up his running whenever he can – be it in high-profile charity runs or simply short sprints around his local park. He stays in shape by running, and he can often be seen jogging around London's Hyde Park in his spare time. As for many people, he says jogging helps to clear his head and focus his mind, as well as making him let go of life's everyday stresses. In May 2003 he faced a stress and challenge of a different kind, however, when he took part in a six-mile charity run in Hyde Park in aid of Help A London Child, 'Feetbeat 2003'. Set to quicken the pulses of both his fans and himself, Will attended the event dressed in simple jogger's shorts and vest-top, wearing his competitor's number 5390. But, as always, he certainly stood out from the crowd. Having done a lot of training beforehand, Will came a very respectable twenty-second out of the 5,400 runners in the race, and was tremendously proud of his achievement.

But May wasn't simply a flurry of songwriting and charity runs. As spring hesitantly ventured into summer, devastating news reached the Young family – news which would knock all other thoughts out of Will's head. On 4 May 2003 he learned that his brother, Rupert, had been arrested and charged with assault following an attack on a thirty-five-year-old chef called Kawa Ghareeb in central London.

Television floor manager Rupert and two friends were arrested on the morning of 4 May and questioned for ten hours after the unprovoked attack, which left Mr Ghareeb needing four stitches in his head. It was claimed that Rupert resisted arrest – and then tearfully begged police not to tell Will what had happened.

Rupert told the police that he had passed out after drinking too much in Tokyo Joe's bar in Soho. He fell over and hit his head and woke up in St Thomas's Hospital sometime later. As he left casualty, he claims that Mr Ghareeb walked towards him chanting and waving his arms. 'He was just coming at me. He had hold of myself. I hit him. I was still very disorientated. There was lots of shouting and I fell to the floor,' he says.

Rupert asserts that a 'rugby maul' then took place, and he and his friends all ended up on the floor: they were arrested shortly afterwards.

A Metropolitan Police spokesman confirmed Rupert's arrest: 'At 6.55 a.m. a twenty-four-year-old man was arrested on suspicion of assault. The twenty-four-year-old has been bailed to return to a London police station on a date early in June.'

But the very day after the alleged attack, Mr Ghareeb told the *Mirror* newspaper a totally different version of events. When asked about the assault, which took place outside the Tate Gallery in Pimlico, he claimed: 'I was walking home on my own when three lads came at me and started beating me. One in particular was very persistent – he was wearing a white T-shirt and had a plaster on his face. When they started hitting me I tried to walk away. I was screaming for help and trying to run away, then the most persistent one hit me from behind. It must have been something big and heavy because he cut me across the head and I needed four stitches. He hit me so hard he knocked me out. The next thing I remember is waking up in an ambulance.'

He then continued, 'I still feel in a lot of pain. I don't know why they picked on me. They screamed things at me but I couldn't tell what they were saying because I was so frightened. I don't know whether they were being racist or not, but they were out to get me and I gave them no reason for that.'

The trial was held at Middlesex Crown Court in July 2004. When questioned in court, Rupert claimed that being the brother of someone famous has made him an easy target for people and put him under a lot of strain. 'At times I have been called gay and shouted at by builders. In fact, myself and Will were attacked in a club once,' he told the court. 'We as a family all try and stay positive. But there are times when members of the general public seem to act in a strange way around him or myself.'

The prosecutor Ivan Clarke claimed that Rupert was 'in a somewhat arrogant mood' that night and attacked Mr Ghareeb without warning and used him 'like a punch bag'. He also questioned why three men would attack one.

However, QC Stephen Brassington, who was acting for Rupert and his co-accused friends David Kennedy, twenty-six, and Anis Shlewet, twenty-five, said that Mr Ghareeb had exaggerated his injuries, possibly to better his chances of criminal compensation. He also branded Ghareeb a 'gold digger' for selling his story to a newspaper. Brassington told the court that Rupert was guilty of being a 'drunk, arrogant, young fool', but he was not guilty of assault.

Mr Kennedy, of Shoreditch, east London, and Mr Shlewet, of Chelsea, west London, both denied the charge of causing actual bodily harm and both were eventually cleared of assault. For Rupert, however, the verdict was not so straightforward.

When summing up, Judge Timothy Lawrence told the jury that the case was simply a matter of who they believed – Rupert or Mr Ghareeb. But the jury failed to reach a verdict over Rupert's involvement in the first trial, and the Crown Prosecution Service was given a week to decide if there should be a retrial or if the case should be dropped.

The CPS ultimately opted for the retrial, and so the case continued. A second trial date was eventually set for November, and once again the jury heard how Mr Ghareeb was returning from a night out when he came across Rupert and friends. A row erupted and it is claimed that Rupert then chased Mr Ghareeb, who fell and injured his head.

Rupert denied the chase ever took place, but this time

round he did plead guilty to using abusive or insulting words or behaviour, which is a public order offence. In response to this guilty plea, Judge Fabyans Evans gave him a conditional discharge. The judge also ordered that a 'not guilty' verdict be entered on the affray charge.

Outside the court, after the trial, Mr Ghareeb commented: 'If he doesn't go around smashing other people's heads in then justice has been done.' For both Rupert and Mr Ghareeb, it was finally the end of a long-running case, which had dominated the headlines and garnered massive media coverage.

But in June 2003, all that was still to come. Still stunned by the developments in his brother's life, Will could do nothing but struggle on with the workload of his burgeoning career. The second album was still topping his list of priorities, and Will was thrilled at how it was turning out: 'I have worked with some varied writers this year and I feel in a way that this is what this year's been all about,' he reflected. 'It has been fun working with so many different people – they all differ artistically, but it is also a challenge to meet and create a working artistic environment with so many different people on a week-to-week basis.'

Yet as excited as he was about the album personally, Will was also focused on providing good material for his fans. Despite his glam new lifestyle, with celeb-packed award ceremonies and paparazzi-dodging now part of his day-to-day schedule, he hadn't forgotten how he'd achieved his coveted position – and he was determined not to let his fans down.

'People voted for me in *Pop Idol*,' he said. 'They put me in this position. I think there's a bit of a responsibility there and I don't think I've fulfilled it yet. I'm predominantly a soul-jazz singer, and that's what I always did on the show. And the last album really wasn't either of those things.

'It's interesting, people come up to me and say, "I've got your album, I love it, I voted for you, but when are you going to sing something a bit more Will?"'

As it turned out, the second album would be a showcase for just that kind of sound.

CHAPTER ELEVEN

Moving On And Moving Up

Will's first major gig of 2003 took place on 18 July at Killerton Park, near Exeter, Devon. He guest-starred at the concert, which was held in aid of Positive Action South West (a charity for which Will is the patron, and for whom he organized fund-raising events even while at university).

The event aimed to raise money for the AIDS/HIV research charity, and over 6,000 fans turned out to watch Will's inspiring performance, which was complemented by an acoustic band. For Will himself, it was a very special night. 'I am so happy and excited to have been asked to sing at the Exeter Festival,' he said. 'I have such fond memories of Exeter from my slightly mad university days, which only seem like yesterday, and it's great to be performing on my own for the first time in the place where I gained the confidence to perform.'

Will really sees his university town as a home from home. In particular, he loves the Cathedral Green, which is one of his favourite places of all time; while at university he was always to be found there, chilling out and enjoying life. The gig was something of a homecoming for the Exeter graduate, and the fact that it was raising money for Positive Action South West was also a real bonus, especially given Will's long-standing relationship with them.

Will psyched himself up for the gig by playing a CD of some of his favourite artists, and the strains of Grace Jones, Bill Withers and Joan Armatrading got him in the mood. Meanwhile, his warm-up acts – a samba band called Street Heat and a soul singer called Sarah Bennett – got the audience revved up. Sarah was first spotted by a member of Will's management team, when she performed at a Prince's Trust concert. And as soon as Will heard just one of her songs, he wanted her to play at the gig, considering her to be the perfect act to complement his later performance.

Just before Will took to the stage, he got a huge boost in the form of a letter and pin badge from the Mayor of Exeter, which stated that he was now an Ambassador for Exeter. 'I was thinking that they didn't really want me as an Ambassador, particularly if they'd seen me drunk in the student union!' Will joked.

The singer finally appeared on stage at around 9 p.m., and crooned his way through his hits and album tracks like 'Evergreen' and 'Lovestruck', covers of some of his favourite songs, such as Stevie Wonder's 'Superstition' and Sting's beautiful 'Fields Of Gold', and even treated the thrilled audience to some brand new material from his forthcoming album. He finished off the gig with a rendition of 'You And I' – his favourite song from the last tour.

All in all, the star performed for a lengthy two-and-a-half hours and enjoyed every second of it. 'I don't think I've ever played in front of a crowd who were so up for it,' he said with a grin. 'It really lived up to my expectations. I wanted it to be that type of atmosphere; very relaxed, very joyous and a real laugh. There wasn't anything over the top. I didn't want to come out to fireworks and a big build-up.'

Once again, Will garnered some great reviews. 'The little minx threw in some very saucy dance moves, as if we weren't salivating enough already!' commented one cheeky critic, while the *Exeter Express and Echo* reflected: 'Last night, people had converged from all over the world to witness his developing talent. Well before Will arrived on stage, the fans were chanting the name of their idol. When he arrived on stage, Will opened with new song "Ticket To Love". With his tight rhythmic band stirring up some soulful sounds, more new songs followed, all in a similar jazzy pop style, including the uptempo swing of "Dance The Night Away" and the slow ballad "Alibi Of Love". As the light receded, fans held aloft lighters, glow sticks and even wore flashing bunny ears, adding to the atmosphere.'

But it was down to Will to sum up the evening. 'The first half was amazing and when I went into the second half I did not think it could get any better, but I was totally overwhelmed. The crowd were amazing,' he said, smiling.

On 12 October 2003, after nearly a year's wait, Will's very patient fans finally got to hear his brand new single, 'Leave Right Now', when it was showcased across a number of radio stations. And although it may have been some time coming, Will felt that it was worth the wait. 'The great thing about taking time out is it has enabled me to explore my creativity,' he said. 'There's a real intensity in this track which taps into basic human emotions – the clash between the heart and the mind. What I love is that my voice carries the melody of the song. It's not overproduced and the simplicity really highlights how emotional it is. Vocally, "Leave Right Now" really shows how much I've moved on. And the more I sing the song, the more I like it, which I think is a sign of a good song.'

It was accompanied by a stylish video which saw a smartly dressed Will looking mean and moody in a swanky art gallery. 'The idea behind the video is that we're at an art gallery opening. It's very elite, very smart and very dignified,' explained the video's director, Kevin Godley, who has also directed videos for music veterans U2 and Bryan Adams. Kevin knows a thing or two about being a pop star himself, as he is a former member of both Godley and Creme and 10CC. He continued: 'Everybody [in the video is] very snooty and posey and dressed to the nines and Will is singing to the camera – the camera being the point of view of somebody that we never see. What he's doing is a catalyst for a chain reaction of trouble that actually works its way around the whole gallery. We're attempting to do it all in one shot because it's a point of view and the point of view doesn't cut.'

But filming an art gallery opening wasn't quite the timid affair you might have imagined. In fact, when it came to the moment when Will is thrown to the ground by a burly security guard, a stunt coordinator had to be on set to ensure that he wasn't injured during the dramatic scene. 'It's getting more and more aggressive as it goes on,' Will revealed during the shoot. 'No one knew there was a nasty side to Will Young. The song lends itself to a bit of aggression and a bit of intensity, so that's what's coming across. It's got a real reality sense about it which I haven't seen in that many videos. It seems very fresh and it's performance-based but it doesn't feel like people are acting. I guess that's the key really, because it's believable.'

The entire video was filmed on a handheld camera, which added to the natural feeling of the film. The video had to be shot in one take and the cast and crew ran through it over twenty times to ensure that they captured exactly what they wanted. A group of actors were hired for the shoot, including *Where the Heart Is* star Kelly Wenham, and as the video had a proper story to it, Will also got the chance to show off his own drama skills.

It was quite a physical and draining shoot, so Will was happy and relieved when it was all finished. A huge cheer went up from the cast and crew when the slick take was played back. 'It didn't take as long as I thought it would,' said a jubilant Will, 'and it's nice to be working with a director who knows when he's got what he wants. I'm really pleased. I think it's going to look fantastic. I know Kevin is pleased, and everyone else is so I will wait and see the result.'

Kevin had relied on a gut feeling to let him know when he'd got the take right, and he was confident that they'd nailed it. 'It feels like it went well in my bones. I think we got perhaps four really good takes. The last two specifically were very good. Touch wood.'

As Will zoomed around the country promoting the single, he admitted to one interviewer that he was glued to the new series of *Pop Idol* – which Michelle McManus eventually went on to win – and joked about how tough it is for people to take part. 'I think it's great. I mean, I'm completely addicted to it, but then I suppose I'm a bit biased, aren't I? God, I can't believe people go through that!' he laughed.

Will also revealed that his new album, *Friday's Child*, was near to completion, and that all in all he had written around fifty potential tracks. Of the final twelve that had been chosen, he had co-written eight and was immensely proud of what he'd achieved.

Having been out of the spotlight for so long, Will was suddenly back with a bang around the time of his new single, but despite great reviews, he was apprehensive about how 'Leave Right Now' would do. But those in the know were confident it would be yet another winner for the Hungerford lad. Industry magazine *Music Week* commented: 'This swooning ballad has the hallmarks of some of the true classic love songs and is a sumptuous showcase for the best voice so far to emerge from reality TV. With radio joining in over the last week, a smash seems assured.'

However, much controversy surrounded the release of 'Leave Right Now', when it was revealed that not enough copies of the single had been printed to meet the incredible demand from the public. After selling over 37,000 copies on its first day of release, it soon became obvious in the days that followed that people were having problems getting hold of the track. This meant that it sold just 8,000 on its second day of release; it was now trailing behind Shane Richie's 'I'm Your Man', which looked set to take the top spot in the coming Sunday's charts.

When Will appeared on Chris Moyles's Radio 1 show on the Tuesday of release week, Chris's sidekick Dave told Will: 'With regards to the single, we've had a common thread on the email system about people saying they have been trying to buy it, but they haven't been able to get it because they have been selling out – and this is the case in Croydon, St Albans and also on the Isle of Man.' Will replied: 'That's good; my housemate sent me a text in Oxford Street saying the same thing.'

But Dave then rightly commented: 'It's not good really: if people want to buy it and it's not in the shops, then that's going to stuff you.' Chris added, 'You have got to learn these things. That's a distribution problem.' To which Will replied, 'I'll have a word.'

He clearly did, because the next day Will's record company BMG released a statement admitting that there was a shortfall in the number of singles on sale, because several record stores hadn't ordered enough copies ... for fear that reality-TV-show stars were no longer big sellers.

HMV's head of press, Gennaro Castaldo, acknowledged that they didn't anticipate the huge demand. 'This is the strongest week-one demand for a single that we have experienced all year and a small number of stores were taken a little by surprise and ran out of stock quicker than expected. However, they now have copies of the single back on the shelves to cater to this huge demand from fans,' he said.

When just 7,000 copies were sold on the Wednesday, the tabloids ran stories of conspiracy theories, claiming that people were purposely trying to stop Will from getting another number one.

More copies of the single were pressed urgently – but fans were still having problems getting hold of them on the Thursday and Friday. However, by Saturday the shops were fully restocked and the record-buying public were once again able to get their hands on the song. There was a last-minute rush of purchases as desperate fans snapped up the record, and soon the single was back on track to make it to the very top of the charts. By the time Sunday came, 'Leave Right Now' had managed to shift over 117,702 copies (5,000 more than Shane Richie's charity track) and another fantastic number one was secured – impressively, Will's fourth to date.

November soon arrived and saw Will scoop yet another award, when he beat off competition from Robbie Williams and Justin Timberlake to take home the Favourite Album award at the National Music Awards. Although he was once again nominated in the Favourite UK Male category, he didn't mind losing out to his friend Gareth Gates.

In early November Will performed a special acoustic set for 200 lucky fans in The Late Room bar in Manchester. Fans were able to win tickets via Will's official website for the bash, which was organized to celebrate the launch of the album *Friday's Child*, and it was a chance for them to get genuinely up close and personal with Mr Young.

In the run-up to *Friday's Child*'s release, officially scheduled for 1 December, once again Will started to worry about how the album would be received. *From Now On* had been critically acclaimed, but Will was concerned that people were still going to judge him off the back of the *Pop Idol* phenomenon. What he wanted to prove once and for all was that he was a talented songwriter who was in it for the long haul – as well as being a brilliant singer. 'To be honest I think it's just people's opinions and you've got to respect that. I think a second album is hard whoever is doing it, but I think there was a notion of, "Well, what's he going to come out with?" In a way it was like do or die, but I didn't mind that. I think everyone has that at some stage in a job, and you have to prove what you're made of.'

And he certainly did that. Even Simon Cowell couldn't hold himself back from saying complimentary things about the album and commented, 'I have to say, Mr Young, this is a *great* record. You sound great on it. Good production. I like it a lot.'

Pretty soon it was proved that Will's fans felt exactly the same way. *Friday's Child* scored Will his second number one album, selling 202,000 copies in its first week of release; it went double platinum after just three weeks having sold 648,000 copies. By the end of the first month of release the record had shifted over 859,000 copies, and many reviewers were openly acknowledging that the impressive collection far exceeded their expectations.

A thrilled Will remarked: 'I think the most important thing was for me to take a year out and take the music seriously, and show that I was taking it seriously, and to come back with something that I was a hundred per cent proud of. That's all you can do. And I am so proud of the album. The way it's selling and the way that people have reacted to it is really fulfilling.

'You need to push yourself and the music needs to mature, and I think I needed to show that there was more substance to me than just being a great singer. I think doing the writing has helped that a lot. It was important to do that. It's great to get recognition from the industry, but also you want to feel fulfilled in yourself. And I've definitely felt that recently.'

His voice had also improved, thanks to him finally

RIGHT: Will with his beloved older sister Emma. His family are hugely supportive of his career and, according to Will, help to keep him grounded.

LEFT: Will's twin, Rupert Young, arrives at court in July 2004 for his trial for alleged assault. The brothers are extremely close.

LEFT: The honour of a lifetime: Will performs at the Queen's Golden Jubilee Concert at Buckingham Palace, accompanied by legendary guitarist Brian May from Queen.

British idols for every generation: Will proudly stands alongside (from l-r) the infamous Ozzy Osbourne, former Spice Girl Emma Bunton, 'Sex Bomb' Tom Jones, and national treasure Cliff Richard, at a photo call at the very special gig.

Will and Gareth share a giggle on stage in September 2002, dispelling persistent rumours that there is a bitter rivalry between the two.

Will makes his West End debut in December 2002, in *The Play What I Wrote*.

Will performs to a televised audience of over 20 million, as he and *American Idol* winner Kelly Clarkson duet on 'Ain't No Mountain High Enough'. The pair were later to sing on the globally broadcast *World Idol*.

With his extraordinary voice and talent (*opposite page*), it was never going to be long before the industry accolades came flooding in. Will receives his first BRIT Award (*right*), for Best Breakthrough Artist; collects his third National Music Award from hostess Amanda Holden in 2003 (*centre*); and, in 2005, adds to the collection with a second BRIT, presented by Hollywood actress Minnie Driver, for Best British Single for 'Your Game' (*bottom*).

Will speaks at the launch of a new website for children who are experiencing domestic violence in April 2005. Since winning *Pop Idol*, he has endeavoured to use his prominent position to help many charities, including Mencap, Women's Aid, Positive Action South West and the Prince's Trust.

Will chats casually with the Prince of Wales, for whom he has performed on several occasions, at the annual charity Party in the Park concert in July 2004.

Will at the 2005 Elle Style Awards, where he won the award for Best Male Music Star (*top left*); in a clinch with good friend Rachel Stevens (*above*); and sharing a laugh with cast mate Bob Hoskins, Will's co-star in his debut movie, *Mrs Henderson Presents*.

OVER PAGE: From one idol to another: Will duets with his hero James Brown. The original Pop Idol more than holds his own against the original Godfather of Soul.

managing to ditch cigarettes, and he was happy to be able to show off his impressive new range on *Friday's Child*. 'I think the voice has improved,' he observed. 'I gave up smoking, and my range has gone up as a result, so it's good news. My falsetto has come on a lot and I'd like to work on that even more. I think if you're a good singer you can con people, you can do the easy work, but you need to push yourself. I always used to think, "Impress them, belt it out!" But on this album, there are some very quiet songs and that intimacy can draw people in, so that's something I've taken on board. The voice is in good shape, definitely.'

The *Sun*'s Dominic Mohan was so impressed with the album that he was moved to print an unprecedented apology to Will, part of which read: 'A fierce critic of processed musical spam I may be, but in Will I can now recognize a true talent. I'm not just talking ballads – he's written one of the year's best slices of teary pop in "Leave Right Now" and has managed to cement himself as a serious artist with mass appeal. It's a clever little song which has straddled radio and video station genres.'

Mohan went on to praise Will's singing abilities and even his 'decent' personality in the apology. In particular, he admired Will's unwavering determination to become a credible, respected artist, over and above making a quick buck by cashing in on his sudden celebrity status. As Mohan says, 'Like his music or not, for that he deserves respect.' Unlike many other talent-show winners, Will was all about the music – his passion for which had pushed him to audition for *Pop Idol* in the first place – and now that he was making a splash in the music business with his impressive self-penned tunes, many critics were finally starting to sit up and take serious notice, Mohan included. He commented: 'Will is now being re-evaluated.'

Luckily for Will, all the signs were that that re-evaluation was one hundred per cent positive – something which the singer couldn't help but be pleased about. Will admits that, even though he tends not to listen to what the critics have to say, success feels even sweeter because so many people thought he would be a one-album wonder. 'I think in any job, and particularly in something creative, if you're driven to prove critics wrong, you're doing the job for the wrong reasons. The wonderful and equally infuriating thing about music is that everyone's got an opinion. So I think you should try and do what you want to do. And when people come round to it, it's wonderful. But the critics aren't my driving force. If they are you lose the reason why you're doing things. On this album I've tried to let the music and the performance do the talking, and that's what you're judged on. I tend to keep my mouth shut and get on with the job!'

At the end of December Will took part in a huge event that brought *Pop Idol* winners from around the world together in a super-competition. *World Idol* was filmed in London and aired in the UK on Christmas Day. Will found himself up against Alexander Klaws from Germany, Guy Sebastian from Australia, Heinz Winkler from South Africa, Alex (Alicja Janosz) from Poland, Diana Karzon from Pan Arabic, Jamai Loman from the Netherlands, Kelly Clarkson from America, Peter Evrard from Belgium, Ryan Malcolm from Canada and Kurt Nielsen from Norway.

The show was screened in all the participating countries and, just like in *Pop Idol*, viewers had to call in and vote for their favourite singer. Representatives from each of the countries got to be a part of the judging panel. Simon Cowell was chosen to represent the US, where he adjudicates *American Idol*, while Pete Waterman did the job for the UK.

Will performed 'Light My Fire', and despite getting fantastic feedback from both Pete and Simon on the night, several of the judges were less than kind, with one even suggesting that he needed to take singing lessons. Not that he minded, as unbeknown to the judge in question, Will was already taking singing lessons as part of his quest to keep on improving his voice.

'I've just started singing lessons again,' he revealed shortly afterwards. 'I became a bit arrogant in thinking that I could just do it. I turned up in a studio recently to do an acoustic version of the new single "Your Game", and I thought how well my voice naturally goes into these bluesy areas. Then I realized I haven't sung for two months. I thought, "I need some more singing lessons." My breathing has gone out, my placement was bad, and I really wanted to work on my falsetto, to get it brighter. I'd like to control my vibrato a bit more. There are some vowel sounds that I want to work on. So yes, I must get my arse into gear. Especially if I'm touring and promoting new material.'

The results show of *World Idol* was screened on New Year's Day 2004. Despite Will's new singing lessons and his delivery of a fantastic performance, former plumber Kurt Nielsen, from Norway, was the overall winner. He was crowned World Idol after impressing audiences with his rendition of U2's 'Beautiful Day'. But it wasn't all good news for Kurt: while Australian judge Ian Dickson compared him to a hobbit, the ever-cutting Simon Cowell told him: 'If this competition had been on radio you'd walk it. The problem is you are ugly.'

Nevertheless, the global audience voted Nielsen top, with America's Kelly Clarkson placed second and Belgian Peter Evrard third. South Africa's Heinz Winkler was in fourth place and Will came in fifth.

It was only after the show that Will revealed what he *truly* thought of taking part. 'Oh, that was just awful. Dreadful! I just didn't want to do it,' he said. 'It wasn't that I felt above it. I just didn't see why I was going back into a competition. I thought it would be better to do it and represent the country than to be slagged off for not doing it. Maybe I just didn't take it seriously enough.'

Yet again, Will had had another great year. On top of everything else, 2003 saw him buying his first house – in London's trendy Notting Hill – and he spent a lot of time furnishing it and making it feel like his own. 'It's strange having a mortgage. My father said to me, "Things are different when you get a mortgage," and it's true. I can't wait for the day I pay it off,' Will said of his new pad.

Up until his house purchase, Will had been living with his good friend Mary in her west London flat, as he had been since leaving uni. But having his own place meant that he finally had somewhere he could go and totally be on his own, locking the rest of the world outside. With the press interest in him still growing rapidly, it was important for him to have somewhere that was *his*, where he felt totally safe and secure. And as two of his closest friends from university moved in, he always had someone to turn to when the going got tough.

Having his own home also gave Will space to think, and he reflected on what a circus his life had become. When people are being demanding of you 24/7 it's difficult to find a moment's peace, but Will has his ways of coping. Although he's not a particularly religious person, he is very much into spirituality, and it is this that brings him peace during difficult times. 'I do have my beliefs. I think the *Pop Idol* experience was a big spiritual thing for me,' he says. 'I don't like to talk about it that much because I think it's a personal thing. The last year and a half I have become a lot more spiritual in trying to find reasons for things. Where did this voice come from? I'm really lucky, but why am I lucky that I do a job that I love? Where did that come from? It does make you think a bit more.'

But sometimes Will takes his desire to stay grounded a little too far. It seems no matter how rich he becomes, some old habits die hard, for Will still can't shake off the memories of being a poor student. Even now, he'll try and save a few pennies if he can. 'I bought sunflowers the other day, and the woman on the stall asked for an autograph. So I said, "Okay, and how about a discount?" She couldn't believe it,' he says. 'It's being a student, it never leaves me. It's quite a luxury to go to a supermarket and buy the Taste the Difference range.'

With the fresh year of 2004 upon him, Will was looking forward to taking some time out to think things through. He confessed that the process of being in the public eye, along with everything he'd been through in the past year, had helped him to toughen up and realize a lot of things about himself. 'I think I've grown up a lot and probably become a lot harder. But in a necessary way, not in an unpleasant way. I think one thing I have done is I've lost a bit of perspective, because I've been so involved in writing and everything. I used to have a great sense of perspective, but I've slightly lost that at the moment in terms of putting things in their place. Working really hard on something, you do get involved and you do really care about it. So I'm looking forward to taking some time out again and coming back chilled out and happy.'

Is it ever possible for him to hide away and truly forget he's famous? 'I do, actually,' he reveals. 'And it's probably a really pretentious thing to say, but I did particularly in 2003 because I was out of the public eye a long time, and people are fickle. We are all fickle as people, and if you don't see people around, you stop recognizing people. You do kind of forget, and then people come along and talk to you and you're like, "Oh, hello."'

Will was looking forward to getting back into the studio in 2004, and was building up all sorts of other plans too. 'I'm really excited, to be honest,' he enthused. 'When your confidence is up and things are going well I think it's important to get back into the studio. There's nothing better as a writer than to do stuff and have people enjoy it. So I want to get back into the studio and go on tour in May, and maybe do a small theatre tour. That would be great.'

CHAPTER TWELVE

That Skimpy Pair Of Swimming Trunks

The new year got off to a great start for Will, with his album at the top of the charts. By now it was a certified triple-platinum record, having sold over one million copies. Meanwhile, sales of his single 'Leave Right Now' had topped 400,000. Will was also crowned winner of *Heat* magazine's Sexiest Body poll, pushing the omnipresent David Beckham into second place and Hollywood superstar Jude Law into third. Will's good friend Rachel Stevens topped the girls' poll, with Kylie and Beyoncé in second and third respectively.

Things were still going immensely well for Will and his popularity showed no sign of waning. Even when he was taking time out from work he was still being written about regularly, and it seemed that the public couldn't get enough of him. But he did have a slight concern about how the public perceived him. 'I have a bit of a problem with people calling me "nice". Nice denotes boring,' he explained. 'It's a bit wet and I'm not a wet person. I'm a very strong person. I wouldn't describe myself as "nice", because I think that's like "cute". But I treat people well, and I expect to be treated well back, and that's the way I choose to lead my life – sometimes I feel I should apologize for it!'

As far as the fame side of things was going, he was enjoying it and was proud of the fact that although his job title had changed, he'd still managed to stay the same person, despite everything. 'I'm making a point of enjoying it more,' he revealed. 'I say to myself, "I've bought a bloody house, this is great!" I'm a lot further ahead than I thought I would be, but I think that's because I'm more relaxed. People are always like, "How's your life changed? You must have loads of famous friends now." Not really! The main thing that has changed is that my job description is "singer". When I'm visiting new countries I love writing that on the form, because that's been my dream since the age of nothing. The other change is being famous. I don't think I've changed a great deal. Maybe I'm stronger than I was. I guess I'm more honest as well. I'm certainly a lot happier in myself.'

On Monday 12 January came some news that was to make Will even happier. It was announced that he had been nominated for another BRIT award, and would be battling it out with Badly Drawn Boy, David Bowie, Daniel Bedingfield and Dizzee Rascal for the Best British Male Solo Artist gong. Mr Young's career was going from strength to strength, and the continued recognition from the industry meant a lot to him.

But when the big night came on Tuesday 17 February, despite being hotly tipped to win, Will lost out to Daniel Bedingfield in his category. But the night didn't go to waste, and a cheery Will still had a fun time catching up with old friends and enjoying the odd glass of champagne at the swanky BMG aftershow party.

The next task in Will's busy schedule was another single release. Following the smash hit 'Leave Right Now', 'Your Game' was revealed as the second single to be taken from *Friday's Child*. It was accompanied by a stylish video, which was shot in Australia, and is up there with Will's favourite videos to date. 'I really enjoyed "Light My Fire" as well, actually,' he recalls. 'And I love "Friday's Child", but it was really hard work. I love doing videos – they're the things I get very excited about,' he says.

Michael Gracey and Peter Commins, who also directed Will's winter 2004 arena tour, directed the 'Your Game' video. 'Basically the video gets bigger and bigger and there are different scenes. It starts off with myself, the band and this amazing reflective floor,' explains Will. 'That for a lot of videos would be the end, so to start from there kind of says that it's going to be really big.'

Will had a cinematographer and a lighting designer on set to ensure that the stage set-up was perfect. '[Having] both a cinematographer and a lighting designer is an amazing luxury to have on a production, because it's two people and all they're looking out for is how the light is playing,' said director Michael. He went on, 'It's an amazing avenue for your work released worldwide. You get calls from people who have seen the latest [video] and you can't really comprehend that [outcome] when you're on set just making something.'

But the video wasn't only about lighting designers and shiny floors – it was a choreographic tour de force too. Ashley Wallen, who would go on to do the choreography on Will's winter 2004 tour, explained: 'We've had rehearsals for a good week and we started off at about ten dancers, then we had another twenty come in, and today we're ending up with about fifty dancers in total, which is a bit of a hard task for me but lots of fun.'

The results were amazing, but the shoot wasn't without its problems. As David Wakely – director of photography on the video – explained, the shoot was done in a bit of a rush and the watery flooring caused them no end of trouble too. 'We've all worked together in a very short time, which I guess has probably been the biggest challenge,' he said. 'I think the best job has been the wardrobe. I haven't seen anything got together quite so quickly. The backgrounds are amazing. They were done in a very short time. We were looking for a glossy background and we tried wetting this pond liner and it was just leaving streaks. So we tried making it into a pond and it just works so well with Will stepping in and splashing around in it. It looks fantastic so we went with it. And of course, a lot of our time is spent in it with Will.'

Indeed, Wakely has nothing but praise for the singer. After the shoot he raved: 'Will is wonderful to work with. He seems like he's been doing it for a very long time. Much longer than I thought.' From the results of the video, it's clear to see that everybody's hard work paid off.

Following on from the video shoot, Will had to do yet another round of interviews to promote 'Your Game', and while he isn't quite as passionate about doing interviews as he is about making videos, he understands that it's part of the job and it's necessary if you want to make people aware of a new release. 'You do a video for five days and then you do a photo shoot and an interview and another photo shoot and then you go on holiday and you forget that you are supposed to be a singer. And that's what it is to be a pop star. It's a business,' he says. 'You can focus on the writing and the singing and that, but then you have to just go out and bloody sell it. And you have to have something that you are proud to sell.' Fortunately, all his creativity over the past year had resulted in material that Will was very pleased with.

But, of course, the press attention on Will isn't just focused on his latest musical offerings. Does he ever get bothered by the other things that are written about him in the press? 'I do if I read it, so I try not to,' he reveals. 'I think if it is really constructive, then I have the right people around me who will tell me anyway. The rest of it you don't really need to hear, because it will always stick with you somewhere and it kind of stumps your freedom. So I try and work it like that and then if I've really f****d up someone will tell me, and if not I'll just get on with it.' He continued, 'I've never pretended to be perfect – so there's less danger of being caught out. I mean, I can't imagine what it is I'm going to do wrong, but I'm sure I'll do something – apart from what I already do wrong on a daily basis. And I guess it will get into the papers. But at least I'll be able to turn around and say, "Well, I never said I was perfect."'

For his fans at least, though, it really seemed as if Will could do no wrong. 'Your Game' went straight to number three when it was released in March, having been pipped to the top spot by Usher's 'Yeah' and DJ Casper's 'Cha Cha Slide'.

In May came perhaps Will's proudest achievement to date. He received yet another award for his mantelpiece when he was honoured with a coveted Ivor Novello gong, accolades which celebrate the work of British songwriters, composers and music publishers. He picked up the Best Song Musically and Lyrically award for 'Leave Right Now' – which he co-wrote with Francis Eg White – at the swanky Grosvenor House bash. Will was delighted that his songwriting talents, which he had spent so much time honing over the past year, were being recognized – and by such a prestigious organization.

Will took to the road once again in May and June of 2004, this time performing on his first ever solo tour. Having previously played huge arena venues, he wanted to give his fans the chance to be a touch more intimate with him, so chose smaller theatres around the UK for the gigs. Will said of the shows: 'I have been looking forward to this all year – getting back on stage and singing. To be able to perform in theatres should make every night unique. Obviously any hecklers will be thrown out!'

Kicking off on 22 May and spanning twenty-two dates,

tickets were said to have sold out quicker than for Madonna's last tour, and the frenzy was justified. It was hailed as a huge success and Will loved every second. 'I love playing live, and I love singing with live instruments because it makes such a difference,' he enthused.

As for the critics, the *Sun* couldn't say enough good things about him, raving: 'Will Young proved he's our biggest male star next to Robbie Williams as he kicked off his British tour. In trademark ripped jeans and cap, Will captivated the sell-out crowd at St David's Hall, Cardiff, with his mix of charisma and shyness.'

The *South Wales Echo* was equally impressed and equally forthcoming with the comparisons to established and well-respected stars: 'There's a reason critics are calling him the next George Michael. Not only can the boy sing, but when it comes to stage presence and charisma, he'd put the majority of so-called "authentic" musicians to shame. He performed all his hits as well as songs from the acclaimed [second] album, including "Your Game" – and the audience loved it.'

What wasn't there to love? Selecting seventeen songs with which to delight the crowds, Will put on an unforgettable show. The set list contained a majority of original self-penned songs from the albums, but there were also a couple of covers – quality songs which Will had made entirely his own, such as his rousing rendition of 'Love The One You're With', and a show-stopping version of Outkast's 'Hey Ya' (perhaps an unlikely choice for the Pop Idol to cover, but one which demonstrated his ability to identify a hit melody at fifty paces and then blow it out of the water with his versatile voice). 'Evergreen' was still included; being such a pivotal song in Will's career, the nostalgia factor always brought a smile to fans' faces, as well as taking everyone back to those early momentous days – giving them a chance to reflect on how far Will had come since then. In all, it certainly made for a night to remember.

Those fans who weren't lucky enough to get tickets for Will's theatre tour got a second chance to catch him in action when he went on a festival tour around the UK in summer 2004. The Liverpool Summer Pops concert, Stowe Music Festival and Eastleigh Summer Music Festival were just some of the shows he played at as he made his way around the country. But Will didn't just wheel out his old routines for these latest gigs. 'We've kind of had a massive turnaround to create this completely different show [for the festivals],' he revealed enthusiastically. 'There's a little acoustic bit now, it's a bit more chilled out. Which is nice for summer.'

As ever, Will's versatility was something he was keen to exploit. And the relaxed atmosphere of the festivals suited him down to the ground. As Will explained, 'I think if you can do it, you should do diverse things. It gives the audience a different show and different things to see. And if the music lends itself to both styles, then you should do it. The thing with me is that I'd be at my happiest singing with an acoustic guitar, you know what I mean? These shows are quite like that, so I'm very happy. I just hope people don't get too bored because it's so mellow.'

Come June, it was time for Will to buy himself a bigger awards cabinet when he scooped yet another accolade and was presented with the Silver Clef Award for Artist Of The Year. In the very same month, Will was invited to perform at the prestigious Olympic Torch Ceremony – which featured stars like Jamelia, Ozzy Osbourne and Rod Stewart alongside Mr Young – held to mark the grand final of the Olympic Torch Relay.

Tens of thousands of people turned out to watch the six-hour event, which took place in front of Buckingham Palace on London's famous Mall. Will got the chance to realize yet another of his dreams at the concert, when it was arranged that he would perform a duet with soul legend James Brown. Brown had kicked off his music career back in 1965, with the same song on which he was to duet with Will – the world-famous smash 'Papa's Got A Brand New Bag'. Since his sixties debut, Brown has experienced a roller-coaster career which has seen highs and lows (including a well-publicized two-year jail stint for assault), and to this day is still referred to as 'The Godfather Of Soul'. He is one of the most respected musicians in music today, so Will was exhilarated to be sharing the stage with such an icon. The Pop Idol and the soul legend belted out the classic hit to a rapturous reception: over 70,000 people watched the show, and the rare duet was a real highlight.

The collaboration was a particular thrill for Will, as he had long been a fan of the man often described as 'the hardest-working man in show business'. As both musicians cherish the genres of soul and funk, the pairing was an ideal match. 'It was really, really great singing with someone you're a massive fan of and who is a living legend,' Will said of his collaboration with Brown. 'It was really, really wonderful, a real moment where I just thought, "You've really got to enjoy this." Singing with people like James Brown gives you the motivation to keep on doing it. It's people like him who drive you on. He told me I should wear more hats – that's the key to success. I said if I'd known it was that easy it'd be wonderful.

'I've never enjoyed a performance so much. You can't help but move to that kind of music. And with him, he's so charismatic. We didn't rehearse or anything. Actually I watched it back the other day and it looked more polished than it felt. We didn't know what the hell we were doing. We just kind of danced around together. We were running down the Mall and it's just hysterical. It's, like, *James Brown*, and it's one of those surreal moments where you think, "What's this job about?" It's fantastic.'

June was a very busy month for Will, as it also saw the release of the third single to be taken from *Friday's Child*, the title track, which reached number four in the charts. 'I went for that one, because all of the singles so far have been really different,' he explains. 'The first one was a classic pop ballad and the next one kind of moved me on a bit musically and was more funk and soul. This one is probably the most musical track I've done really. It's just kind of chilled-out soul. And it just shows another side of the album. But the video is great and I think it's had a good reception on the radio. It seems like people are enjoying it and that's all you can wish for.'

The accompanying video caused quite a stir as it featured Will in some skimpy swimming trunks looking taut and toned; perhaps unsurprisingly, it swiftly became one of the most played videos on music-request channels.

The video was filmed in the UK over two days. 'It's basically my progression from learning to swim to becoming an Olympic swimmer to finishing the English Channel,' Will explains of the short film. For the shoot, the singer was provided with a swimming coach called Hillary, who oversaw his swimming techniques – and she was very impressed with the skills he displayed. 'He's done very well indeed. I'm very proud of him. I'm sure he'd make an excellent lifeguard,' she said. And what did Will think of such high praise? 'I'm not one to brag, but I think I could make a lifeguard,' he agreed good-naturedly.

But did Will worry about exposing so much flesh in the promo? You might have thought that a gorgeous pop star such as Mr Young would be utterly happy with his looks and more at ease than the rest of us in stripping off – but you'd be wrong. When you live your life in a goldfish bowl with people constantly commenting on how you look, it can begin to get to

you. Will admits that he frets about his appearance –
especially because he's under the scrutiny of the public and
the press at all times. He describes his legs as 'chicken legs'
and regularly worries about his wonky jaw. When he was
eighteen, he turned down the opportunity to have it broken
and re-set (perhaps because it would have meant that he
wouldn't have been able to talk for ages), but that didn't mean
it wasn't still an abiding concern for the modest star.

Yet on the plus side, Will does admire certain aspects of his
physiognomy – well, one aspect in particular. 'I have always
really liked my bum,' he says with a cheeky smile. 'My bottom
is very pert and high. And I have good ankles. My mum has
always been known as having a great ass so I think I must get
it from her. I want more comments about my bottom from
people, so if you see me in the street feel free to say something
nice about it. I want to win Rear Of The Year because I have
got a great arse!' (Little did Will know it at the time, but just
over a year later, in September 2005, he would achieve that
very ambition, being crowned as the male Rear of the Year at
a ceremony in Knightsbridge.)

It seems his confident attitude was in attendance during
the 'Friday's Child' video shoot. Will was certainly keen to
dismiss talk of possible body doubles. 'No, I didn't need a
double, even though it was bloody cold, because I've got quite
a large penis,' he told one shocked interviewer. 'I'm quite
pleased about that and I'm not worried, otherwise why do you
think I'd do a Speedo video? It would be ridiculous.'

And despite looking incredibly toned in the video, Will
claims he didn't do any special workouts to ensure that he
was looking his best. 'I kind of do a lot of stuff anyway, so
maybe it gave me some more of an incentive to look vaguely
presentable. I shaved my six-pack thinking, "I'll get that out
more." I did sort of breathe in for the entire two days.'

On 3 July, Will made his debut appearance at ultra-hip gay night G-A-Y at London's Astoria – the same day that London's annual Gay Pride march took place, where thousands of people flocked to the streets for a huge celebration. 'I wanted to do a proper gig. I've been to see some friends do shows at G-A-Y and they sing to backing tracks with dancers. And I thought that would be cool, but it is quite a special day and it's the first time I've done it, so I really wanted to do a proper concert.' As Will revealed, it was a big show for him. 'They asked me if I wanted to do it on that day and it seemed kind of right really. It's the first time I've played there and it seems right to do it on a day that is more commemorative than other days. A bit more celebratory.'

On top of the G-A-Y gig, Will also performed a fantastic five-song set at London's Party in the Park concert in July, which was watched by over 100,000 people. His cover of Outkast's 'Hey Ya', which he had previously showcased on tour, went down a storm, as did 'Light My Fire', 'Friday's Child', 'Leave Right Now', and his cover of the Paul McCartney track 'My Love'. Proving his popularity with the royals is still going strong, Will sat with Prince Charles to watch some of the show, which included performances by The Corrs, Natasha Bedingfield, the Sugababes, Lenny Kravitz and Busted.

In August Will added two more awards to his ever-growing collection, when he picked up the Favourite UK Male Vocalist and Capital Album accolades at the Capital Awards in London. He got everyone talking when he arrived at the ceremony, thanks to an unusual new haircut that was incredibly short at the sides, but long at the top and back like a modern-day mullet. When he picked up his first award he decided to make a reference to his hair, joking that it was a bit eighties … he wasn't wrong.

Collecting his second award, the Capital Album Award for

Friday's Child, he commented: 'I was really pleased to win the first award, but this one has made my day. It's the one I really wanted to win. When you have given one project everything you have got and it's given you two breakdowns, it's great when people appreciate what you have done. I was joking about the breakdowns, by the way!'

Will caused another fashion stir when he turned up at the nineteenth birthday party of his management company, 19, at the Royal Albert Hall in London. Sporting a bowler hat and a black-and-white stripy jumper, he looked more like a French mime artist than a bestselling singer. He partied the night away alongside the likes of David and Victoria Beckham, Rachel Stevens and Gareth Gates, and performed his hits 'Leave Right Now' and 'Your Game', as well as the title track from his album, *Friday's Child*, to the assembled elite guests.

Money-wise, all of Will's hard work was obviously starting to pay off, as he was placed at number eighty-five in the *Sunday Times*'s annual 100 Richest People List, with a rumoured fortune of £4 million. The politics graduate from Hungerford had certainly come a long way.

But Will still wasn't letting his wealth and status go to his head. 'I won't allow a job to change the way I want to lead my life and what I think. Maybe just recently I've been going through a bit of a time when I have found it hard to hang on to a bit of individuality and what it's like to be me, but I think that happens to everybody. Age twenty-five is a bit like going through teenage years again. But it's all part of the test, isn't it? You've just got to keep going.'

And there was definitely no danger of him turning into a diva, with a huge entourage attending to his every whim. 'I don't have a massive entourage. I don't think mine is challenging Jennifer Lopez's yet, but maybe one day,' he said, smiling. 'I think we can probably stretch to an assistant stylist at some stage.'

By now, it had been over two years since he shot to fame on *Pop Idol*, and when asked if he was keen to shed his *Pop Idol* tag, he replied, 'I wouldn't say shed it. I think the only thing, maybe, was for me to shed the image of what people thought of people from that show. I think, you know, I wasn't really the norm to come out of that show anyway. People kind of had an idea that where I am now is kind of where I was going to end up. I'm very proud of where I came from and very proud of the show. I would never sit down and say, "Damn that show, it was awful," because it gave me my break and I will always be massively grateful for that.'

On the subject of his staying power, he comments: 'You couldn't have predicted it and it's obviously what I wanted to happen. I just think the thing is you just keep on going. It's two things really – not really changing as a person, and I didn't want to do that, and making sure the music is good enough for you to stick around. I have to remind myself that you're very lucky if you do have that, and I'm really pleased that we've got to that stage.'

In August came the news that Will had hoped for ever since his West End debut in 2002. After a lot of hard work and auditions, he landed his first ever film role – as a character called Bertie in *Mrs Henderson Presents*, a movie set in pre-World War Two London. Filming began almost right away on the £10 million movie, which is based on the true story of an eccentric socialite called Laura Henderson – played by acting legend Dame Judi Dench – who bought an old London cinema and transformed it into the Windmill Theatre. Bob Hoskins played the part of Vivian van Damm, a fierce theatre manager whom Laura hires to run her new project. The pair clash over the way things should be done, but ultimately make the theatre a huge success – with Bertie (Will) as their star performer.

In its day, the Windmill became famous for its musical revues and vaudeville acts, which, scandalously, were often performed naked, and needless to say caused quite a stir in 1930s London. The Windmill remained hugely popular during the war and was in fact the only theatre that stayed open throughout the bombing of London in 1940.

Will delighted in his first film experience, saying: 'In the two-and-a-half months [we were filming] I didn't have one bad day at work, which is amazing. I always have bad days, but it just goes to show how much I enjoyed it.' However, he did have one worry about his role ... that he would encounter a bit of a problem when it came to acting alongside a cast full of sexy ladies in their skimpy clothes: he was terrified of getting a 'stirring' at the sight of the sexy showgirls. 'It's ridiculous, but I was worried about getting aroused while we were filming. It ended up not being a problem. I was surrounded by beautiful women, but nothing moved down there at all,' he laughed with relief.

Judi Dench, meanwhile, was hugely impressed by Will's acting abilities, and commented: 'Will Young is ace. He's wonderful. He's perfect for the part and he can act too. And he's the most amazing singer. One only has to see Will as this young man at the Windmill. He does it supremely well.' Will responded to her praise by saying, 'When Dame Judi said I was ace that knocked me over. She's a pleasure [to work with] and having that sort of praise from someone of her standing is unbelievable. I just sat there and thought, "Life doesn't get much better."'

Will also admitted that having got a taste of the thespian life, he now had another acting ambition that he was desperate to fulfil – to appear in cockney soap opera *EastEnders*. 'I'd love a part on *EastEnders*. Definitely. I'd want a hat stall on the market and then I'd work in the Queen Vic at weekends. I'd be the only gay on the Square!'

And, you never know, he might just be in with a chance. As he remembers, 'They once played my single in the background in the café. And they were playing my song on the radio during one of the scenes between Jamie and Sonia. How incredible is that?'

CHAPTER THIRTEEN

What A Performance

Musically, things went from strength to strength for Will in 2004. By October his album *Friday's Child* had sold almost 1.5 million copies, he'd scored a number three hit with 'Your Game' and a number four hit with 'Friday's Child'.

And his new successes meant that he was finally able to put what he refers to as 'that dreadful, dreadful song' – 'Evergreen', which he admits he would never have recorded given the choice – behind him, and concentrate on his newest victories.

'I don't look back on it with bitterness or distaste,' he says of the track. 'I've had four number one singles, sold a lot of albums and won a BRIT. It's all good.

'It was definitely a challenge singing it, but I suppose selling over two million records showed that I did alright with it.'

With 'Evergreen' firmly consigned to the past, Will's next musical adventure was just around the corner. He was asked to contribute to the *Bridget Jones: The Edge of Reason* soundtrack, and recorded a cover of Sade's 'Your Love Is King' for the album. As the film was set to be a worldwide smash – in its opening weekend alone, it took over $8.5 million at the US box office and over £10 million in the UK – it was another chance for him to get noticed in America.

But although Will's record company BMG were still keen for him to attempt breaking the States, Will himself is unsure it's a direction he wants to go in – especially following the comments made about his teeth earlier in his career. 'I've been offered a major deal, but I'm in a dilemma,' he confessed. 'They want me to keep quiet about my private life and, worse than that, they've told me I have to get my teeth whitened and straightened. I thought they were joking, but that is the bottom line,' he seethed.

On 4 November, Will was left distressed when thieves broke into his west London home and stole personal items including private photographs, designer suits worth around £30,000 and, perhaps worst of all, his laptop, which contained lyrics for new songs he had been working on for the next album.

Luckily, however, the police were able to solve the crime soon afterwards. Two men, twenty-four-year-old Sharife El-Whabe and twenty-two-year-old Annis Seddiki, were arrested when they tried to sell Will's personal pictures (which showed him wearing a dress and a blue wig on the set of *Mrs Henderson Presents*) to a national newspaper for £5,000.

During their trial, Judge Deva Pillay said of the robbery: 'At the end of the day it seems to me that those who effectively, by this kind of process, invade the liberty and privacy of subjects which they know is likely to cause embarrassment to those subjects, you must recognize the inevitable consequence is immediate imprisonment.' The pair, who both pleaded guilty to the charges against them, were sentenced to six months' jail each for the 'retention and control of criminal property' and a further six months for possessing criminal property.

The burglary was all the more distressing for Will as he is such a private person. He has been accused of being guarded in the past, but he insists that it's important to keep something for yourself in such a weird business. 'I'm not cagey,' he explains. 'I just think you've got to keep some things to yourself. If you open up everything then you never have anything to yourself. I've always been like that. I mean, I wouldn't tell a friend what my pay packet was. For me it has always been quite rude to talk about money – I've always been brought up to think that. I'm not intensely private but you should keep things to yourself.'

It's for this reason that he appreciates the fact that his fans are by and large polite and respectful towards him. 'It's definitely true that people are more involved in my life. But I like that. And also I think that because they know me, they never invade [my privacy]. Like if I'm eating or something people won't ask me for my autograph, they'll wait until afterwards, and that's really nice,' says a thankful Will.

Towards the end of 2004, Will faced one of his biggest challenges yet, when he embarked on a sixteen-date solo tour, this time playing at some of the UK's largest arenas. Though the gigs followed on from Will's smaller tours earlier in the year, this was to be an entirely different affair. For his first big solo arena tour, Will wanted everything to be done on a big scale. The planning itself was a huge operation, necessitating a creative team with several people on board, each of whom was responsible for a separate aspect of the show. Will himself was involved in everything – including, of course, the exhausting run-throughs that were central to making the tour a massive hit. The singer completed intensive rehearsals in dance studios with his backing dancers in the run-up to the shows, before the group moved on to Shepperton Studios, where they had a replica of the tour set constructed. Will was at pains to encourage a democratic atmosphere where people could contribute opinions, and it seems that this was effective, with everyone making suggestions and coming up with ideas.

As ever, Will's busy schedule meant that time was tight in

the run-up to the gigs. The star of the show himself was only able to rehearse at the very last minute, which necessitated some rather hectic practice sessions for the whole team. But the tricky timing was just one of the dilemmas they faced. There was another, fairly major, problem during the rehearsals at the Middlesex studios – the lack of a stage. It took Will some time to get used to performing on flat floors whilst trying to imagine being raised above the audience for the actual shows. It was all a bit perturbing to begin with.

Ashley Wallen, who choreographed the show from start to finish, agrees that being in the rehearsal process is an utterly different experience to delivering live gigs. For a start, it's always hard to gauge how an audience will respond to a production, and the sterile nature of the rehearsal room simply can't equate with the vibrant atmosphere created by an excited audience. There's just no vibe – as well as no lights, stage, costumes and so on – so rehearsing without an audience always feels slightly odd. But it was a necessary hard slog into which Will threw himself enthusiastically.

During rehearsals, Ashley took a dressed-down Will through his paces and showed him the movements in detail, so that he could get a firm grasp on the routines. Once on tour, Will's concentration was going to be focused on his singing, so he needed to be on autopilot while performing the dance routines. It was a tough brief to fulfil, but Will approached it with his usual upbeat attitude, and was soon throwing the right shapes at exactly the right time, to Ashley's warm approval.

Not everything went totally according to plan during this all-important preparation period, though. One evening during rehearsals, a fire alarm meant that everyone had to evacuate the building, and Will also had to have physiotherapy to take care of his aching muscles, which were feeling the strain of the intense schedule. But as he was soon to discover, all the pain was going to be worth it.

'Bringing a show like this together is a matter of sitting down on a couch with Will and going through the songs in order, and coming up with ideas on the spot that you really have no idea whether anyone's going to take seriously,' says the show's co-director Michael Gracey. 'The thing is, Will takes them very seriously and people take Will seriously, and [because of] that you end up having to do them.'

In the planning stages of the shows, Will had several meetings with both Michael and his co-director, Peter Commins, so that the star could put his own ideas across. On his *Live in London* DVD, Will says: 'I sat down with Michael ... months ago ... and we went through the show and wrote it all down and all our ideas. And to see something really come out exactly how you saw it – if not better – is really rewarding. And it gives you confidence to go on and do more things and I'm very, very proud.'

Michael, too, was thrilled with the finished result. And although the show might have appeared to the audience as a seamlessly put-together affair, with a throughline and a journey constructed from a painstaking thought process, Michael confessed that it wasn't actually produced that way at all. In fact it was something that evolved fairly naturally.

Choreographer Ashley worked closely with the directors in creating the physical numbers for the shows. He took his inspiration for the dance routines from glamorous, vivacious, classic old films. As the show was going to be quite theatrical, Ashley decided to rent some old movies to inform his ideas – in particular, some of the Fosse films. Dancer and choreographer Bob Fosse is world-famous for his work, which includes the choreography for the Liza Minelli smash film *Cabaret* (1972) and the stage musical *Chicago* (1975). The idea was to put a modern twist on the old spectacular routines, capturing the timeless feel, but bringing it up to date.

In keeping with Will's own refusal to be pigeon-holed in the music industry, Ashley revealed that the gigs were anything but your standard 'teenybopper' pop concerts, too. 'There are a lot of theatrics. It's like doing a big musical, but with pop music,' he said enthusiastically.

Will loved this melting pot of inspiration, and from the first few days of rehearsal he could see it all beginning to take shape. In fact, he was thrilled at how it was all coming together. As everyone's aim was to make the show a hit, the work was very focused and productive. But with the directors working hard at realizing their and Will's visions for the shows, and Ashley producing some sizzling, show-stopping choreography for the dancers and Will to perform, there was still another, very important aspect of the show that the team had to tackle: the singing.

Will's friend Joseph Ross, the tour's musical director, was heavily involved in this process. Will and Joseph had been working together ever since Will had won *Pop Idol*, and the input of the singer's musical director was crucial in making the singing side of the shows a success. The years of partnership have resulted in a great working relationship, and the two collaborated closely on the new musical arrangements for the upcoming tour. As Joseph says on Will's *Live in London* DVD: 'How I like to work is to bring something a bit different to how [the songs are] on the album. Myself and Will, when we came to devising the set, we sat down and we talked about which songs would work and the different musicality aspects. We really bounced a lot of music ideas off each other. The good thing is that a lot of the ideas I come up with he really likes, so it makes it a lot easier that he trusts my judgement like that.' Joseph went on to add, 'It's probably one of the highlights of my career so far.'

Unlike other pop stars, who sometimes rely on flash sets and computer wizardry, Will has always put his music first in his career – and that was his philosophy when it came to the tour, too. 'The music always has to be key. When you get to bigger shows you can lose sight of the fact that you have to pay homage to the songs – what people bought in the first place, what drives them to come and see you live – so the singing and the music that's played [are all-important]. And I think we've done that.'

Will appreciates that a big part of getting the music side of things right is down to having a great band with him on the tour, and he has a lot of respect for the musicians who accompany him on stage. Unlike many singers, he is at pains to distance himself from the stereotype of the diva who just turns up, sings, and heads home again. Instead, the friendship he's nurtured with the band really comes across on stage, upping the atmosphere and generally improving the gig, as Will and the musicians joke around and jam together on stage. Will always makes sure he introduces the band at every show, too, partly so that the audience can demonstrate their own appreciation of the fantastic contribution the musicians make to the night, but also as a gesture of his own recognition of their talents.

As for the crew, they found Will a joy to work with, and his enthusiasm for the upcoming concerts quickly spread to the whole team. 'The good thing about Will is he doesn't see celebrity as this all-expenses-paid safari, he sees it as a job [at which] he works very hard,' said co-director Michael. 'And like everyone else, he's on set for long hours, and he shows a lot of respect for all the people that support him and do his tours and are a part of it. It's the fact that he has that professionalism that makes him a real pleasure to work with.'

Meanwhile, co-director Peter enthused: 'When you create something, how it's created comes across. It doesn't matter what the final product is, the environment in which it was created is always something that you can read. And the great thing about Will is that the environment in which it was created is generally a lot of fun. It's something that people enjoy.'

Ashley Wallen particularly likes working with Will, whose dancing is constantly improving, according to the dance expert. Apparently, Mr Young is a 'fabulous student', and Ashley is impressed by how much Will's dancing talents have come on since the choreographer first worked with him on the video for 'Your Game'. When you recall that Will was considered to be the best male dancer on *Pop Idol* (as said by choreographer Paul Roberts), it's good to know that he's gone on to fulfil that early potential.

And it seems that Will is equally impressed with Ashley. 'He's one of the few choreographers who choreograph to the music rather than the beat,' says Will. 'He feels the music. There is so much choreography I've seen where I feel that people just do it strictly "one, two, three, four". Whereas he really listens to it and gets the moves.'

However, it wasn't Ashley up there night after night shaking his stuff with Will on stage – and the singer has just as much respect for his backing dancers, with whom he adored working. Will enjoys having a bit of company on stage, relishing his musical rapport with the band, and he felt that the dancers' vibrancy really boosted the energy and liveliness of the gigs too. Will says of the dance troupe: 'They're beautiful people and beautiful characters, and they're always happy. The *whole* time. I think dancing must be the best job ever. We have a real laugh and it's been a pleasure to get to know them.'

Ashley backs him up one hundred per cent, revealing that many of the tour dancers were the same professionals used for the 'Your Game' video shoot. As that group had produced such fantastic results, neither Will nor Ashley saw any need to alter the line-up once the planned tour had been confirmed, so they didn't bother auditioning for any new ones. As the saying goes, 'If it ain't broke, don't fix it,' and this proved a worthy maxim to follow when it came to the dance troupe involved with the tour.

So what with this dream team of dancers, a pair of well-established directors, his favourite choreographer and his long-time musical director on board, Will's first solo arena tour was shaping up to be something quite special. But the warbler had something else up his sleeve, too. The singing lessons he had started taking around the time of *World Idol* were still a regular fixture in Will's busy schedule – and by now he was really reaping the rewards that they offered. His voice was in fantastic shape, with his tutors, CeCe Sammy and John Modi, quick to sing his praises. 'For this tour we've worked really in depth on his whole range, really preparing him,' said CeCe. 'I think we're going to hear a new and evolved Will Young. We've heard Will at his best and now we're going to hear him at his supreme best.'

'He's a very intelligent artist and what you give him he will take on board and he'll put his own slant to it,' added John proudly. 'He's just developing every single year. His style, his repertoire, his musical identity, his vocal identity, [they're all] just evolving.'

For Will the respect was mutual, and he knew that he'd definitely chosen the right team of people to take this journey with him – not just his singing coaches, but also the band, the dancers and everyone else involved in the tour. He appreciated the fact that the team never treated the gigs as 'just another day job'. For Will the project was crucial – it was the first arena tour he had ever done solo – but everyone else was behind the shows one hundred per cent too, contributing ideas, time, effort and enthusiasm throughout the rehearsal process and beyond. There was a lot riding on it. Everyone wanted the tour to be a huge triumph.

They needn't have worried. The unique fusion of personalities and hard work was to result in some of the best gigs Will had ever performed. But although he was determined to focus on the music and the 'soul' of the shows, he wasn't averse to the odd bit of technical trickery. A big part of the stage shows were the short films, which were shown on massive screens behind Will. During the concerts, for example, the gorgeous 'Very Kind' was performed with 'multiple Wills', using some clever tricks. A film was shown behind Will, which featured six other versions of him, making it look as though he was being reflected around the stage. Will ran through the moves with Ashley numerous times before and after the material was filmed and Peter also gave him some tips.

'We filmed "Very Kind" out in Sydney,' Will said. 'In the show I have to match my movements to what we filmed out there so it looks like mirrors. It's a very hard song to sing and it's just difficult to remember those moves.'

The video was shot against a black screen using six cameras, which all filmed Will from different angles. He had to go over the moves lots of times to get them spot on. If he made a mistake, they had to re-shoot the entire video as it was screened as one take. After filming, Will then had to put in even more time rehearsing, to ensure that he could replicate the moves perfectly on stage.

'Very Kind' wasn't the only highlight of the tour, however – Will had made sure that there were numerous show-stopping moments to delight his fans. In another video filmed for the big screens, this time to be played during 'Over You', he donned a red-and-black jewelled outfit and topped it off with a dodgy moustache and slicked-down hair. The results were stunning – and showed Will in full comedy mode as he shimmied around some glamorous Spanish dancers.

For a third video, Will dressed up as a clown with full make-up and a sequinned waistcoat. He made jokes about hating it during the shoot, but clearly had the time of his life larking about, and once again showed that he has a great future in acting. Michael, who directed the short films along with Peter, was hugely impressed with Will's drama skills, and was full of praise for his professionalism. In Michael's view, not only was Will the composite performer – not just a pop prince but an accomplished all-rounder, with abilities that stretched beyond his vocal talent – but he was also focused and hardworking every time he performed. Equally importantly, he was a lot of fun to collaborate with, too.

Everyone involved with the gigs had different favourite tracks on the tour – Ashley loved 'Friday's Child', CeCe and John liked 'You And I' and 'Leave Right Now' respectively, while Joseph rated 'Love Is A Matter Of Distance'. And Will's favourite? It was undoubtedly the fantastic 'Friday's Child' – for a number of reasons. 'My favourite number is the opening, actually, "Friday's Child",' he revealed. 'It's very understated. I didn't want the show beginning to be, like, "Will flies in on a motorbike," you know! It's so not me as a person. [Instead,] you get these girls dancing and then diving into the water. It's beautiful. The whole thing is sensual and sensitive and just has quality to it. I think it's fantastic. And I don't usually say that about things because

I'm very, very critical about my own work. But you can tell that I really enjoy it. I love it.'

The opening is truly striking – fans who missed the gigs can view the show in all its glory on Will's *Live in London* DVD – and as Will *didn't* fly in on a motorbike, the audience was never quite sure if he was part of the group opening the show on stage or not. This all added to the fans' anticipation and excitement on the night.

As for Will himself, he certainly enjoyed this tour more than any he had been on before. 'I enjoy being on stage now. I enjoy dressing up and getting into those costumes. It's great!' he raved.

The greatly mixed audiences – from kids to OAPs – were treated to a selection of songs from Will's two albums, *From Now On* and *Friday's Child*, and no one left disappointed as he belted out all the favourites, plus a few special additions. Will's main aim throughout the creation of the tour had been to give his fans a night they would never forget. And he was determined not to let them down. As a music enthusiast himself, he's attended lots of gigs – but not all of them have lived up to his expectations. He didn't want his own supporters to have that same disappointment. So as well as all the large-scale aspects of the shows – the big screens, the big sound, the jazzy costumes and the dance routines – Will concentrated on more minor elements too, looking to produce the whole package for the audience. As he himself says, 'You know, the big things will take care of themselves, but the tiny elements are the things that ... even if two people out of 10,000 notice, they have that moment.'

It soon became obvious that all Will and the crew's hard work had paid off, when the first show was a massive success. 'It felt like such a slick show. It felt like we'd done so many shows already, which is very weird. I've never felt like that before. And even watching it back it was very slick for a first show,' said a thrilled Will afterwards.

And the press were every bit as enthusiastic when it came to reviews. The *Manchester Evening News* said: 'Judging by the lusting screams and wolf-whistles of the (mainly female) audience, he definitely has it. Will enters to the soaring funk of "Friday's Child", the titular track of his current album that Jay Kay would sacrifice his extensive Dodgy Hat Collection for. Followed by an entourage of dancers, he wears a bowler reminiscent of *Goldfinger*'s Oddjob.'

And the national papers were also, by and large, very upbeat, with the *Sunday Mirror* commenting: 'While his occasional dance routine is entertaining enough, it's his voice that is really faultless, particularly in his jazz-tinged rendition of "Light My Fire" and slow numbers like "Evergreen". Unfortunately, Will was not quite as slick when he spoke to the crowd between songs ... But while spontaneity may not be [his] strong point, he only has to start singing and this enthusiastic crowd is utterly charmed.'

After all the hard work and excitement involved in staging the shows, such positive reviews were the cherries on top for Will and the team. Critics from the national papers to local rags were raving about the innovative tour. From the technical wizardry to the haunting vocals, the colourful costumes to the charismatic presence of Will himself, every aspect of the show ticked every box. And for the fans – the people about whom Will had been most concerned – the gigs were an experience they would never forget.

Will ended the year by taking part in the biggest musical event of recent times. Along with the likes of Coldplay, Joss Stone, Robbie Williams and Bono, he was invited to appear on the Band Aid 20 single, which aimed to raise awareness for the all-important Make Poverty History campaign.

Twenty years earlier, the organizing duo of Bob Geldof and Midge Ure had put together the original Band Aid, a group of popular musicians who joined together to record a single for charity. But not just any charity – the record was in aid of the dreadful famine which swept Ethiopia in 1984, a humanitarian disaster that needed instant millions if any of the thousands of lives being lost each day in the desert were to be saved. It was reporter Michael Buerk's October 1984 BBC documentary that had highlighted the awful plight of the Ethiopian people to the British public, and Midge and Bob had agreed immediately that something had to be done to ease the suffering. The single 'Do They Know It's Christmas?' was the outcome.

The Band Aid effort in the eighties was a phenomenal success, selling over 3.5 million copies in the UK alone and raising millions of pounds to battle the devastating famine. But despite the massive influx of cash, it still wasn't enough. Geldof went on to organize Live Aid as well, two live music concerts staged simultaneously in London and Philadelphia on 13 July 1985, which featured the best and most famous acts of the time. The huge event raised over £60 million for the relief effort. Tragically, 1.2 million people died in the famine – but millions of lives were saved thanks to the international efforts of many.

Now, in 2004, Midge and Bob wanted to make a similar impact by supporting the Make Poverty History campaign, an international movement that is committed to reducing poverty around the world. Every day, 30,000 children die as a result of extreme poverty, so it was a campaign worthy of every support. Piggy-backing on the media exposure of the original Band Aid's twentieth anniversary, Band Aid 20 was formed, with the aim of highlighting the plight of the world's poorest people and the unjust imbalance between the world's richest and poorest countries. Proceeds from the record's sales were earmarked to combat the HIV and AIDS crisis in Africa, as well as to assist with the relief effort in the Darfur region of Sudan, where war and famine had wreaked devastation. In 2004, the UN described Sudan's problems as the world's worst humanitarian crisis, while the charity Save the Children stated that 92 per cent of people in southern Sudan lived in poverty. At the time of Band Aid 20, the Sudanese crisis was dominating the world's headlines: Midge and Bob responded by channelling all their energies into a charity drive they hoped would have the same incredible success as the original Band Aid. In their efforts, they enlisted the help and talent of Britain's leading musicians – and Will was up there with the best of them.

Recording took place at Air Studios in London, and Will shared two lines with R&B songstress Jamelia. Their contribution forms the musical bridge before the first chorus. Will and Jamelia got on brilliantly on the day, and Will also went on Chris Moyles's Radio 1 breakfast show to talk about the single, where he spoke ardently about the crisis in Sudan and explained just how important it was for everyone to go out and buy a copy of the charity track. It seems his fans were listening to him, for the record stormed straight to the top of the charts; three weeks later, the track had held on to the top spot to become the nation's Christmas number one, having sold over 600,000 copies since release. After Will recorded his part of the historic single, he said, 'It's been a brilliant day. It was incredible to be a part of it.'

CHAPTER FOURTEEN

A Brilliant Year And A Bright Future

Will took another much-needed break in early 2005 and backpacked his way through South Africa, Malawi, Zambia and Zimbabwe. By now, he was becoming a seasoned traveller. 'I've been to Africa a few times,' he revealed. 'You get more of an insight into the country if you get on the buses. It's a bit more grass roots than just flying in and flying out. Africa's the most beautiful, amazing place,' he said admiringly.

Not surprisingly, Will continued to get recognized even in the most unusual places. 'Sometimes the borders can be quite scary and there's always African bureaucracy,' he said. 'Sometimes someone behind passport control can be difficult, but this one woman looked at me and said, "You've been on TV." I was in the middle of nowhere and I couldn't believe it. How did she know that? But that's the power of television, I guess.'

On his return to the UK, Will began work on his third album – and couldn't wait to get started. 'I've been holidaying for the best part of the year,' Will confessed in early March. 'It was very good at the end of last year. Fantastic. But I felt like I needed a bit of a break so I've been away for a while. But now it is holiday time over. Holiday no more for William, and it's back in the studio, which is really good. I'm off to America for a bit and then we'll see what happens. It's one of those processes where you have to get back into the swing of things and hopefully you're inspired. You can't put a time on it. But it's very exciting. I'm enjoying it. I'm just sort of writing and seeing what comes up. Hopefully good music!'

February 2005 brought with it another BRIT awards show, and Will, yet again, had received some nominations – this time in an impressive three categories. Despite missing out on the Best British Male and BRITs25 Best Song awards on the night, Will didn't leave the ceremony empty-handed.

On 11 February, at one of the most glamorous bashes of the showbiz calendar, Will was presented with a gong for the Best British Single for 'Your Game'. His shock was evident when actress Minnie Driver read out his name, and he was seen swigging out of a bottle of beer – and swearing – before heading to the podium to collect the second silver statue of his career.

The victory meant all the more to him as he had earlier been dubious about his chances of success in such a tough category. 'I think it's a funny old category because it's bound to kind of get people's backs up, because I kind of know what my favourite song is and it's none of those, it's Joan Armatrading's "Love And Affection". So it is a bit of a weird one,' he said. Still, numerous UK radio listeners clearly rated 'Your Game' as their top tune of the year, and Will managed to fight off stiff competition from Band Aid 20's 'Do They Know It's Christmas?' George Michael's 'Amazing', Jamelia's 'Thank You', Keane's 'Everybody's Changing', LMC vs U2's 'Take Me To The Clouds Above', Natasha Bedingfield's 'These Words', Shapeshifters' 'Lola's Theme', Sugababes' 'In The Middle', and The Streets' 'Dry Your Eyes' to scoop the award.

'The BRITs was fun. I came back that day from Morocco and it was very strange going from North Africa to the middle of Earl's Court,' Will admits. 'But it was actually not a bad night. I'm not fantastic at awards ceremonies and I find them an interesting idea. But I was very happy to get the award for "Your Game". I was very surprised.

'I was very proud of that song. I think that was quite a turning moment for me. "Your Game" was the funkiest song I've done and the best video I thought that I've done. And it was also the most input I've had into a song and into the whole promotional thing, and it really worked. It was nice to see a bit of a reward. I was obviously very grateful to everyone who voted for me.'

Following his success at the BRITs, Will was named Best Male Music Star at the Elle Style Awards. The swish bash took place at London's hip Spitalfields market and was attended by Kylie, who won the Lifetime Achievement title, Cate Blanchett, who was named Most Stylish Actress and Woman Of The Year, and supermodel Helena Christensen, who was presented with a Style Icon award.

Ever modest and always a bit shocked when he gets complimented on his unusual dress sense, Will denied that he was a fashion icon and revealed: 'I don't like it when people say I have a style. It means I am fitting a mould.' Winning an Elle Style Award is certainly a long way from that egg-stained jumper he wore to his early *Pop Idol* auditions. Yet whether he's winning accolades for his sartorial sense or being dressed down for a fashion faux pas, Will is nonchalant about all the feedback. As long as he feels happy and comfortable, he doesn't mind coming across as a little quirky. He openly admits that he wears some fairly wacky clothes and reckons that he's always had a rather, ahem, curious dress sense. 'Right from a young age I've worn some pretty ghastly things,' he says. 'I have always mixed and matched and always been a bit scruffy. I was forever being told off at school for not having my top button done up.'

Will's unique style was soon on show again, when he donned his glad rags to attend a bash held to celebrate *Marie Claire* magazine's twentieth birthday at Café de Paris in London, where he was chatted up by a succession of glamorous ladies. He went along to congratulate the staff of the magazine, in part as a thank you for their unflagging support since his early *Pop Idol* days.

For Will has never been the kind of celebrity who attends the opening of an envelope in a bid to get free booze and a goody bag at the end of the night. He has always maintained that he would much rather be down the pub with his friends than making small talk with strangers in swanky bars and clubs. That is still true today and he is very careful about which events he attends – he will generally go along only if it is a charity event or something in which he has been personally involved.

In March he made a surprise appearance on *Comic Relief*, to perform Bob Dylan's hit 'Blowin' In The Wind' with Ruby Turner. Jools Holland accompanied them on piano and the performance was hailed as one of Will's all-time bests. 'It was great fun to do actually and it was a very last-minute thing. The Jools Holland Band were great; I really enjoyed performing with them. Jools just rang me up a couple of days beforehand and asked me. I loved it.'

March also saw the release of Will's *Live in London* DVD, which went straight to number one. 'I'm really happy with it; the way it's been directed is great and the way it looks is great. I'm happy with all the extras on it too, and it brings back fond memories for me. My favourite part is the beginning. I love everything about the beginning,' Will said.

As April arrived, Will launched a website called The Hideout – the first ever national domestic violence website for children and young people – at London's famous BT Tower. The website is the creation of the Women's Aid charity, for which Will is an ambassador. He is still as keen as ever to help out the charity whenever he gets the opportunity.

Come 8 May, it was time for another of Will's cracking performances, as he joined other artists – including Cliff Richard and Katie Melua – to sing at the VE Day Party To Remember in Trafalgar Square, London. The event was hosted by the British Legion, the BBC and the Mayor of London to celebrate the sixtieth anniversary of VE Day. Will got into the spirit of the event by performing two forties' hits – the Andrews Sisters' 'Boogie Woogie Bugle Boy Of Company B' and Cole Porter's 'Love For Sale'.

These various activities aside, however, Will spent most of early 2005 working on his third album, an as-yet-untitled project. With over 1.5 million copies of *Friday's Child* sold, there was a lot of pressure to come up with a follow-up which was every bit as impressive.

Once again he worked with ex-Alisha's Attic singer Karen Poole, as well as Paul and Ross Godfrey from Morcheeba and Blair Makichen, with whom he co-wrote 'Your Game', amongst others. He also headed off to America's glamorous west coast to work with esteemed songwriters and producers there.

But while he found releasing *Friday's Child* stressful due to expectations, he was feeling more nervous than ever about his upcoming third release. 'Success does breed anxiety. Annie Lennox told me that it doesn't get any easier,' Will said. 'The record company always wants a new album tomorrow. I probably wouldn't be ready in two years – but if things go well, the third album might be out by the end of the year. What's worrying is that I know you need to take risks to move on. It was a risk to take a year out and write the second album and I know that I will make a few mistakes along the way, but you have to keep taking chances if you want to survive.'

In June it was announced that Will's film debut was to get

its first screening at London UK Film Focus – a three-day celebration held to promote British film and talent to an international audience – alongside forty other of the best new British films. The film's director, the well-respected Stephen Frears of *Dangerous Liaisons* and *High Fidelity* fame, has praised Will's acting and singing skills, and a huge buzz surrounds the movie prior to its nationwide cinema release.

Meanwhile, Will landed himself another acting role, this time in *Foley and McColl*, a new TV show created by the men who were responsible for *The Play What I Wrote*, the show in which Will made his West End debut and a guest appearance back in 2002.

June also saw Will hit the headlines for something entirely unconnected to either his acting or music career. Though he's proved on numerous occasions that he's never backwards in coming forwards when it comes to trying out new trends, onlookers were visibly stunned when Will showed off a shocking new haircut for the first time. The singer attended the launch of new online magazine *Phamous69* in June and revealed a freshly shaved head. Although he does have the looks to carry off the severe new look, numerous fan websites called for him to grow back his brown locks – and even Will himself admitted that he regretted his new look. But, as ever, there wasn't the time for regrets as Will's busy schedule pushed on relentlessly.

July brought new demands as Will sang for over 60,000 people at the G8 concert in Scotland – staged at Edinburgh's Murrayfield Stadium – performing alongside the Sugababes and Snow Patrol, as well as many other artists. The G8 concert was held the day before the G8 summit – also taking place in Scotland – when the world's most powerful political leaders, from the USA, Canada, Britain, France, Germany, Italy, Japan and Russia, met to discuss ways to eradicate world poverty and to tackle the important and worrying issue of climate change. The concert was part of Live 8, another brainchild of the indefatigable Bob Geldof. Leading on from the achievements of Band Aid 20 at Christmas time, Bob had decided to use the G8 summit as a focal point for raising awareness of global poverty. As he had realized back in the eighties, one charity single, despite its tremendous success, was not enough to make a real difference on the world stage. So with the impact of the 1985 Live Aid concerts at the forefront of everyone's minds, as the media publicized that event's twentieth anniversary, Bob decided to stage the Live 8 concerts in July 2005. The aim of Live 8 was not to raise money, but to raise awareness of global poverty in the hope that the G8 leaders would, under pressure from the public, cancel third world debt and double aid to the world's poorest countries, enabling them to start anew.

On 2 July, concerts were held simultaneously around the world in London, Berlin, Rome, Philadelphia, Paris, Johannesburg, Tokyo, Moscow and the Eden Project in Cornwall. An estimated three billion people around the globe watched the awe-inspiring shows, which featured an incredible line-up that boasted many of the biggest artists in the world. Madonna, Elton John and Coldplay took to the stage in London's Hyde Park, while in Philadelphia Alicia Keys, the Black Eyed Peas and Destiny's Child were joined by superstar presenters like Will Smith and Salma Hayek. The climax of the incredible concerts took place four days later on 6 July, in Edinburgh, at Will's G8 gig.

As well as performing the One Giant Leap/Robbie Williams hit 'My Culture' with One Giant Leap themselves and Neneh Cherry, Will also took to the stage with his old duetting partner James Brown, for another rendition of 'Papa's Got A Brand New Bag'. Will was ecstatic that he got to perform with

Brown for a second time, and named the performance as the highlight of his day.

And it seems the event wasn't just a success for Will personally. Due in part to the pressure applied by the Live 8 gigs, the G8 summit did achieve unprecedented agreements, including a £28.8 billion boost to African aid, and the cancellation of the debts of eighteen countries. Though the various deals fell short of what many campaigners had hoped for, Bob Geldof acknowledged the progress, paraphrasing words first spoken by Winston Churchill by saying, 'I wouldn't say this is the end of extreme poverty, but it is the beginning of the end.' Will was delighted that the campaign had had such a positive impact on these essential issues.

Aside from the G8 concert, summer 2005 saw Will embark on yet another sell-out solo tour. Ever the experimenter, this time round he decided against playing the traditional arenas, in favour of more unusual outdoor venues such as Leeds Castle in Kent, Beaulieu Motor Museum in Southampton, Chatsworth House in Derbyshire and Stirling Castle in Scotland. 'I've got summer shows throughout July,' said an excited Will before the tour kicked off. 'It's the same kind of thing as we did last time which I really, really enjoyed. I love the vibe of them and so we're not going to change too much from the last summer. A few little things here and there. But I'm really looking forward to it.'

Of course, Will's experience on stage since summer 2004 did inform his creative choices for this latest set of gigs. As he explained, 'We have done an arena tour since last summer and added a brass section – which I love. I will also be testing out a few songs [during the summer festivals] that might make the third album. It's a good opportunity to see how the tracks go down. *Pop Idol* will always be a topic of conversation, but I think I have now moved on. The second album sold twice as many copies as the first and we wouldn't have been able to do anything like this current tour two years ago.'

However, Will admitted that performing outside can play havoc with your voice. 'It's a lot harder to sing outdoors. You warm up your voice and then go out into the cold night air. I was in Morocco and it was so cold my throat was tightening up. The only solution is to have lots of hot water on hand to drink. It's not very rock 'n' roll but it sure helps.'

But it turns out that it might not only be the weather that's affecting the quality of Will's voice. Although he originally gave up smoking back in the spring of 2002, he was pictured in the papers with a packet of cigarettes in August 2005, proving that he is still battling his nicotine addiction to this day. In 2002, Will promised to make a donation to charity if he was ever caught smoking again – it's not known if he's followed through on that promise, but he has admitted that he hates smoking and that it affects his voice. What with Will's über-professional attitude to his career, hopefully it won't be too long before he ditches the harmful habit, and concentrates instead on developing that extraordinary voice of his.

And the voice was certainly what it was all about as Will hit the road for the summer shows. Will's choice of quirkier venues prompted a journalist to ask what kind of venues he preferred playing. Will gave a very diplomatic reply, saying, 'I like them all for different things really. The outdoor ones are very relaxed and there's always a great atmosphere. I like theatres because of the intimacy and I love the buzz of the arena tours.'

The fifteen-date tour lasted from 1 July until 31 July and produced some of the most talked-about gigs of the year. To the delight of fans, as Will had promised he showcased some possible new album tracks on the tour – 'Ain't Such A Bad Place To Be', 'Cuba', 'We're Rolling', 'Madness' and 'Think It Over'.

Will was keen to get more new songs written while he was

on the road. 'I'm making a point of writing more songs on the tour. I want to keep the process going and I'm hoping the tour and venues will inspire me,' he revealed.

As was now becoming the norm, the critics adored Will on stage. The *Liverpool Echo* said of the show, 'Throughout the set there were real highlights with "Light My Fire", and a fabulous encore of "Friday's Child" and a cover of "Love The One You're With". At one point the gaggle of girls looking up to the stage threw Will a couple of cowboy hats, which he wore while strutting around the stage, making you wonder if this was going to be a scene from *The Full Monty*. But we would have had fainting women everywhere if that had happened. All in all, he showed himself to be a born entertainer.'

So the summer 2005 concerts were a huge success – although Will did have a slight mishap during the Manchester gig in Tatton Park, when his lucky pants went missing, making him late for his big entrance on stage. The panicking pop star searched desperately for them for ten minutes, before changing his aim and looking for a replacement pair instead. But as time was ticking by, in the end he had to admit defeat and go on stage in a spare pair – which were kindly provided by a member of his band.

In August, fans got a treat when Will auctioned off some of his personal possessions on eBay for the three organizations of which he is a patron – Mencap, domestic-violence charity Women's Aid, and the AIDS charity Positive Action South West.

The booty included some of his famous hats and shirts, and a quadruple-platinum disc he was presented with for his album *Friday's Child*. 'I'd like to get as much money as possible for the charities I support, but every little bit helps,' Will said. 'It should be good fun to do it this way. I hope people are supportive.'

In the end the eBay auction made over £20,000 for the

charities – with several items going for over £1,000, as bidders upped the stakes in their desire to get their mitts on the Will goodies. The singer's shoes from the final night of *Pop Idol* raised £1,160, while his old Wellington school shirt went for over £500. And it seems Will's footwear is a bit of a passion for his fans – his Puma trainers cost one devotee over £1,330. Meanwhile, the swimming theme of the 'Friday's Child' shoot had clearly proved a hit – Will's swimming hat was auctioned off at nearly a grand. Topping the price list, however, were the *Friday's Child* quadruple-platinum disc (£2,605), Will's infamous Trilby hat (£2,000), and a Will, Gareth and Zoe tour T-shirt, which went for an astonishing £3,000. Will was delighted at his fans' fabulous fund-raising efforts.

Incredibly, it's been just four years since Will first began his *Pop Idol* journey, but he's come a phenomenally long way in that very short time. Unlike many pop stars, he makes sure he retains a lot of control over the direction his career takes, and he doesn't make decisions lightly. 'People think, "Oh, poor Will." They think, "He's married to this process so they will make him sing puppet-on-a-string remixes for ever." It's not that rigid,' he explains. 'People don't say, "Do this, do that." They do listen to what I say. Maybe I will look back on certain things and think, "I can't believe I did that," but I don't believe I will. The advantage of *Pop Idol* is everyone knows who I am. Nobody can change that.'

But Will isn't planning world domination just yet, despite his fame. In fact, he is more determined than ever to resist being morphed into a stereotypical pop ideal by executives in the music industry. 'Kylie and Madonna are brands, and I find that really scary. I wouldn't do that,' he says.

Though Will is undoubtedly a hugely popular star, his time in the spotlight has also taught him that you can't be liked by everyone, and that there is always someone waiting in the wings to throw an unpleasant comment your way. By now, he has got used to being criticized, and the occasional barbed comments simply don't bother him any more. 'You have to be positive in life. There are so many challenges. You need to take things on in an optimistic light or you'll just fail. I believe you can take people's negativity and use it to drive yourself,' he says. 'You turn it around and turn it into strength to prove them wrong. I think that's the way to deal with nastiness and criticism. If I'm walking along the street and someone shouts abuse, I just wave and think, "Thank you very much. I'll be waving at you when I get another BRIT!"'

Those famous feet are still firmly on the ground, and it's going to take a lot to throw him off balance. 'I don't think it's going to be wild parties, drinking and rock 'n' roll that derail me,' he says with that crooked smile. 'If I do them, it's because I want to, not because I'm living up to an image. I have been through my identity growing-up thing. I am really happy with who I am. Even when I went into the competition, I never thought, "I want to be famous and go to premieres and ride in a limousine." I just wanted a chance to sing.'

And the music remains Will's number one priority. He's under no illusions that it is his talent which got him where he is today, and he's determined never to lose sight of how lucky he is to possess that extraordinary voice. 'If you can move people in any way then that's a really special thing. Even if you only move one person, it's a real gift and you should always treasure it and use it accordingly, not abuse it,' he explains seriously.

As for the future, there is still America to consider. It's almost seen as a natural progression that once you find fame in the UK, you try your luck in the tough US market, where the audience is much greater and worldwide success is almost guaranteed off the back of it. But Will remains in no rush to try to conquer the US. 'No plans at the moment,' he says. 'Again I think it's one of those natural developments. There'll hopefully be a right time to go over there and do a bit of work, but it's very nice to know that people appreciate my music elsewhere.'

Although Will's musical future is incredibly bright, true love still evades him, though he says he would love to meet the man of his dreams. While he likes his own company, he does get lonely at times, and says he feels most isolated when he's stuck on his own in a beautiful hotel room abroad, with no one to share it with. A relationship is certainly something he would like. 'I'm quite romantic and don't really meet that many people I like,' he reveals. 'I think people think I'm playing the field, but I'm really not. I'm very much ready for a relationship now and I'm keeping my eyes open, but it will be a very momentous day when it happens. I have never had a serious relationship, so I need to be a bit more proactive about it, although I'm not really sure how to do that.'

Understandably, Will is wary of people trying to get close to him because of his fame, but he reckons he's good at spotting fickle men. He trusts his gut instincts and thinks he's a really good judge of character. 'I believe I would know if they were trying to be with me because I am famous,' he says.

Yet, hard though it is to believe, it seems that one of the best-looking men in showbiz isn't inundated with indecent proposals, despite his well-publicized singledom. 'I don't get many offers, to be honest, which isn't good for the old ego,' he says forlornly. Let's hope the coming years are a bit more fruitful on the flirtation front for Mr Young.

But how about life in general – is he still comfortable with the pop-star lifestyle? 'Yes, I'm very comfortable with it,' he says. 'I think it's because this is something I've always wanted to do, so I half-prepared myself. And *Pop Idol* primed me well because it was a sink or swim process. Although it was a very quick rise [to stardom], we were trained on the way up.'

Will has had several years to get used to the idea of fame now. Does he ever feel like he's out of his depth and get the urge to leave the stress of celebrity behind? 'I do, actually,' he confesses. 'I'm kind of a thinker, so I'm always thinking, "What a bizarre job." It's like all things really. You have wonderful moments where you think, "This is the best thing ever," and others where you think, "What am I doing? Let's give it all up for a day job." It is a job and I think people are surprised when you describe it as that but, you know, you're still earning your living. The thing is you're doing something that you enjoy as your job. In one sense that makes it fantastic, and in another it makes it very personal. But I quite enjoy that I have a job where you can come up with an idea at three in the morning.'

When asked where he sees himself in ten years' time, Will jokes, 'Modelling clothes for a catalogue and having my own line of cashmere cardigans! But hopefully still singing. And hopefully still very happy with a good pert bottom, because that doesn't go until you're forty, apparently.'

As for Will feeling comfortable in his own skin, it sounds like he's got it sorted. As he muses on all the incredible changes in his life – from politics student to international superstar, from a boy who loved running to an award-winning songwriter – it feels like the right time for him to reflect. And he seems to be happy with the way things are turning out. 'I think I've kind of got back to life pre-*Pop Idol*, in terms of, like, me as a person. I think back in terms of what I was doing … It feels sort of like a different life,' he says. 'So in that sense it does feel really weird. But as every day goes on I feel more and more myself again, and I think that's really cool. I don't feel famous in the slightest. It's really funny.'

Discography

Singles

March 2002: 'Evergreen'/'Anything Is Possible' – number one
June 2002 (re-entry after thirteen weeks on sale): 'Evergreen'/ 'Anything Is Possible' – number forty
June 2002: 'Light My Fire' – number one
October 2002: 'The Long And Winding Road' (with Gareth Gates) – number one
November 2002: 'You And I'/'Don't Let Me Down' – number two
December 2003: 'Leave Right Now' – number one
March 2004: 'Your Game' – number three
July 2004: 'Friday's Child' – number four

Albums

October 2002: *From Now On* – number one
July 2003 (re-entry): *From Now On* – number thirty-five
December 2003: *Friday's Child* – number one
July 2004 (re-entry): *Friday's Child* – number seven
April 2005 (re-entry): *Friday's Child* – number twenty-three

At the time of writing, *From Now On* has sold over 770,000 copies to date. *Friday's Child* is now five times platinum, with sales of over 1.5 million.

DVDs

March 2005: *Live in London* – number one

Timeline: *Pop Idol* Songs

Initial auditions

For the show's producers: 'Until You Come Back To Me' (Aretha Franklin)
For the judges: 'Blame It On The Boogie' (Jackson 5)

Second round auditions

'All Or Nothing' (O Town)
'Up On The Roof' (The Drifters)
'Fast Love' (George Michael)

Final fifty televised heat

'Light My Fire' (The Doors)

Week 1 – Your Own Pop Idol

'Until You Come Back To Me' (Aretha Franklin)

Week 2 – Christmas Songs

'Winter Wonderland' (Bing Crosby)

Week 3 – Burt Bacharach Songs

'Wives And Lovers'

Week 4 – Movie Songs

'Ain't No Sunshine' (Bill Withers)

Week 5 – Abba Songs

'The Name Of The Game'

Week 6 – Big Band Songs

'We Are In Love' (Harry Connick Jr)

Week 7 – Number Ones

'There Must Be An Angel' (The Eurythmics)
'Night Fever' (Bee Gees)

Week 8 – Judges' Choice

'Beyond The Sea' (Bobby Darin)
'I Get The Sweetest Feeling' (Jackie Wilson)

The Final

'Light My Fire' (The Doors)
'Evergreen'
'Anything Is Possible'

Set Lists

'Will and Gareth' Tour (Autumn 2002)

'Ain't No Sunshine'
'I Get The Sweetest Feeling'
'Don't Let Me Down'
'Ticket To Love'
'It Takes Two' (with Zoe Birkett)
'Over You'
'You And I'
'Signed, Sealed, Delivered (I'm Yours)'
'Light My Fire'
'Evergreen'
'The Long And Winding Road' (with Gareth Gates)
'Let's Stay Together' (with Gareth and Zoe)

Positive Action South West Concert (18 July 2003)

'Ticket To Love'
'Cruel To Be Kind'
'Lovestruck'
'Dance The Night Away'
'Alibi Of Love'
'Roxanne'
'Over You'
'You And I' (acoustic version)
'Fields of Gold'
'Light My Fire'
'Time Enough'
'Lover Won't You Stay'

'Superstition'
'Evergreen'
'You And I'

Small Theatre Solo Tour (May and June 2004)

'Stronger'
'Out Of My Mind'
'Dance The Night Away'
'Very Kind'
'Friday's Child'
'Light My Fire'
'Hey Ya'
'Love Is A Matter Of Distance'
'Evergreen'
'Over You'
'Going My Way'
'Love The One You're With'
'You And I'
'Your Game'
'Leave Right Now'
'Ticket To Love'
'Free'

Arena Solo Tour (Winter 2004)

'Friday's Child'
'Out Of My Mind'
'Love Is A Matter Of Distance'
'Light My Fire'
'Very Kind'
'Save Yourself'
'Dance The Night Away'
'I Love You More Than You Will Ever Know'
'Free'
'Evergreen'
'Over You'
'Stronger'

'Love The One You're With'
'Leave Right Now'
'In The Stone'
'You And I'
'Your Game'

Outdoor Venues Tour (Summer 2005)

'Your Game'
'Out Of My Mind'
'Very Kind'
'Think It Over'
'Madness'
'Light My Fire'
'Free'
'Fever'
'Lover Won't You Stay'
'Time Enough'
'Ticket To Love'
'Leave Right Now'
'You And I'
'Save Yourself'
'Friday's Child'
'Love The One You're With'
'Cuba'
'Rolling Over'

Sources

Books

Galpin, Richard, *By Public Demand* (Contender Books, 2002)
Galpin, Richard, *On Camera: Off Duty* (Contender Books, 2003)
Solanas, Sian, *Pop Idol: The Inside Story of TV's Biggest Ever Search for a Superstar* (Carlton Books, 2002)
Young, Will, with Marie-Claire Giddings, *Anything is Possible* (Contender Books, 2002)

DVDs

Live in London (Sony BMG, 2005)

Internet sites

www.bbc.co.uk
news.bbc.co.uk/cbbcnews
news.bbc.co.uk/2/low/entertainment/1874237.stm
www.bbc.co.uk/totp/news/interviews/2003/05/27/19598.shtml
www.channel4.com/community/showcards/W/Will_Young
www.ilikemusic.com
www.katieswirls.co.uk/lightmyfire
www.popidolwilliam.co.uk
www.uk.gay.com
www.williamyoung.biz
www.wyoung.co.uk
www.willyoung-a-star.com
www.willyoungcrew.co.uk
www.will-youngonline.com

Newspapers

Daily Record
Daily Express

Guardian
IC North Wales
Sunday Mirror
News of the World
Sun
Daily Telegraph
The Times

Publications

BRITs magazine 2004
Contact Music
CosmoGirl
ES Magazine
Exeter ArtEd
Heat
GQ
New!
OK!
Pop Idol tour programme
Radio Times
Smash Hits
The Sunday Times Magazine
Time Out

Radio

Capital FM
Metro radio
Radio Kent
Smash Hits radio

Television

Breakfast with Frost
Channel 5
GMTV
Richard and Judy
This Morning

Index